Modbury Tales

Trevor Cree

Copyright © Trevor Cree 2025

Trevor Cree has asserted his right under The Copyright, Designs and Patents Act 1988 to be identified as the author of this work.

All rights reserved. No part of this publication may be reproduced, stored in a retrieval system or transmitted, in any form or by any means, electronic or mechanical, photocopying, recording or otherwise, without the prior permission of the publisher.

ISBN 978-1-0682103-4-1

Table of Contents

1.	Introduction	1
2.	Rocinante & Rucio	3
3.	Beginnings	5
4.	Bigbury Bay & Burgh Island	7
5.	Circle	13
6.	Stoke Bay & Noss Mayo	18
7.	Wildlife	27
8.	Kingsbridge	29
9.	The Colour of Money	35
10.	Bantham & Thurlestone	39
11.	Joy!	47
12.	Hope Cove	51
13.	Short, Back and Sides	57
14.	Footpath to California Cross	62
15.	Collectables	67
16.	Footpath to Modbury - May	74
17.	Millennium Sunrise	79
18.	Footpath to Modbury - July	87
19.	Napier Lights	93
20.	Wonwell Beach & Kingston	101
21.	Freedoms and Liberties	107
22.	Prawle Point & East Portlemouth	115
23.	Old John	123
24.	Start Point & Beesands	130
25.	Bluff Hill	136
26.	Errrr-mington	145
27.	Mountain Flower	149
29.	Ermington	150

Chapter 1
Introduction

'Modbury Tales' incorporates twelve short stories, one poem, multiple impressions of a summer in South Devon and photographs that replace a thousand words. It might be described by some as a *'mishmash'* of different genres and that definition seems to sum it up very well. Nevertheless I am very fond of my *'mishmash'* because hopefully it offers a little of interest for all ages.

Few writers, at least as far as I am aware, have combined travel writing with short stories because no doubt they are considered to be different 'genres' and simply do not mix. Like oil and water. And so what better incentive does a particularly independent minded writer like myself need then to purposely swim against the stream of received opinion and do exactly that.

It was never my intention to produce a book during my extended stay close to Modbury in Devon. The whole point of my relocation from Sussex was to reduce my daily living costs by taking advantage of a 'seasonal pitch' for the summer. At the same time my stay offered the opportunity to explore an outstandingly beautiful area of the country that encompassed Salcombe, Dartmouth, a rugged and dramatic coastline and the margins of Dartmoor.

I arrived in Modbury on the 11th March 2022 and without any delay I began to explore the area with an initial day trip to Bigbury Bay and Burgh Island. It was not only a pristine sunny day but off-season as well and the absence of crowds made the visit particularly enjoyable. A few fortunate photo opportunities arose, mishaps occurred and it seemed to me that perhaps one or two others might enjoy reading about my experiences whilst gaining a brief insight into the area.

One visit travelogue turned into two, then three and then four and before long into a short series. The initial response to my writing, and in particular the photographs, was encouraging. I therefore began to share my experiences with others who might not have the opportunity to visit South Devon themselves anytime in the near future. The correspondence was also an opportunity to reestablish contact with former friends and relations that had lapsed over time, as they often do.

As was the case with my previous book, *'Random Journeys - New Zealand'*, writing 'Modbury Tales' was never intended to be a guide book. It was simply the first and fleeting impressions that might resonate with someone else visiting exactly the same location at a different time. Whilst few of us are particularly interested in somebody else's travelogues they do at least allow us to visit places in mind, if not in body. For example, I will never climb Everest nor walk on the moon but photographs have taken me to the summit of high mountains and to the surface of the lunar landscape. And so welcome to South Devon.

Over the years I had steadily built up a stock of short stories that I never widely shared nor published. I decided that 'Modbury Tales' might be the opportunity to do just that. After all, at my time of life, better late than never. Past experience had taught me that producing a print version of a book containing a large number of photographs results in a very expensive end product that is beyond the means of the writer to produce and beyond the means of the ordinary reader to purchase. Furthermore shelf space in independent or chain bookshops is virtually impossible to obtain for a self-published author. In contrast there are no such limitations for digital books where there is infinite global shelf space available and a readership willing to pay a relatively modest amount to be entertained and informed. In 2022 I therefore published 'Modbury Tales' in eBook format but now I have decided to produce a companion print version.

I hope that you will enjoy reading what I have written as much as I have enjoyed writing it.

Chapter 2
Rocinante & Rucio

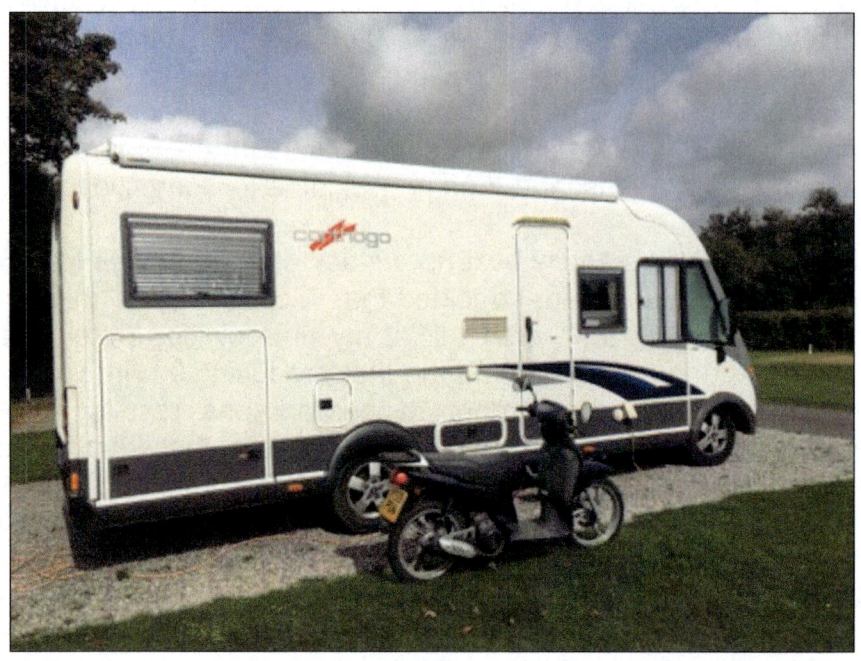

Most motorhome and camper van owners feel a need to give their vehicles a pet name and I am certainly no different. I purchased my vintage 2005 Carthago Chic i47 motorhome in August 2017 and included in the purchase price was a 49 cc Honda moped that was comfortably housed in the very large rear garage. I chose *'Rocinante'* as the name of my motorhome and *'Dapple'* as the name of my moped for very logical reasons. The two names were used by Miguel de Cervantes in his novel *'The Ingenious Gentleman Don Quixote of La Mancha'* that was written in the early 1600s.

I could not have found more appropriate names for my own trusty old steeds because in 2017 I was about to embark on a madcap journey throughout England, Wales and Scotland in order to visit 100 locations that had been chosen by myself completely at random. A journey surely worthy of the unhinged Don Quixote and his faithful servant, Sancho Panza. From Zennor, close to Lands End, right up to Quoyloo in Orkney in Scotland and everywhere in between. No sane person would have embarked on such a journey and so I felt that there was little choice for me but to take on the persona of a modern day Don Quixote who was off to tilt at windmills and join battle with imaginary knights.

Following some characteristic Don Quixote disasters during my initial motorhome travels my less than generous 'friends' soon suggested that *'Nellie'* was a far more appropriate name than *'Rocinante'*. *'Nellie the White Elephant'* most certainly did have a degree of accuracy about it but I would have none of it. *'Rocinante'* the name was and *'Rocinante'* it would remain. I did however change the name of my moped from *'Dapple'* to *'Rucio'*. In the original Spanish language version Sancho Panza's donkey is actually named *'Rucio'* due to its dappled colouring and that is how the English translation of Don Quixote came to use the name *'Dapple'*. However *'Dapple'* never ever sounded quite right to me, rather weak and soft, whilst in contrast *'Rucio'* sounded so much stronger. So from that time on *'Rucio'* it was.

In 1960 the Nobel Prize winning author John Steinbeck undertook a road trip around the United States with his poodle Charley. He stated that he felt moved by a desire to see his own country on a personal level because he had made his career by writing about it in such masterpieces as 'Tortilla Flat', 'Of Mice and Men', 'The Grapes of Wrath' and 'East of Eden'. In 1962 he finally published his account of that road trip in a travelogue entitled 'Travels with Charley: In Search of America.' I had read the book many years ago but it was only now that I discovered that John Steinbeck undertook the journey in a camper truck that he had named *'Rocinante'*. The restored *'Rocinante'* is now on display in the National Steinbeck Center in Salinas, California, and so *'Rocinante'*, *'Rucio'* and myself have very high standards indeed to try to live up to. I hope that we don't let him down.

Chapter 3
Beginnings

The old man was seated in his favourite armchair. He was looking out of the conservatory window to a sea that lay far beyond the rolling Devon countryside and the low wooden garden fence that bounded his property.

Tick....Tock....Grandfather....Clock. It was early Spring and the clear blue skies would still deceive those who might equate that colour with warmth, for a chill wind blew strongly from the east.

His features had an intelligent, almost academic, look that had helped him through life, though not fully deserved. He dressed with military precision each morning although he had never served in the forces. An understated blue tie, cashmere cardigan, white cotton shirt and neatly pressed trousers were his favoured uniform. Todays Telegraph was always close at hand, for that would be his leisurely source of entertainment for the hours to come. *Tick....Tock....Grandfather....Clock.*

Mrs Simpson, his cleaner, came on Monday and Thursday, as she had done without fail for the last fifteen years since his wife had passed away. Mrs Simpson and he rarely spoke, or at least he did not, as she scurried about the place from room to room. From the moment she arrived it was a continuous monologue, not unwelcome mind you, of the comings and goings in the village in the intervening days. *Tick....Tock....Grandfather....Clock.* It reminded him of his wife when they walked along Church Street as she talked and talked while he occasionally nodded assent at whatever she might or might not have been saying. But then it was no different to when he had returned from the golf club and over dinner had informed his wife of the scores that Gerry and he had managed that day whilst she politely threw in a 'Really Dear. How wonderful' before she returned to her sprouts and roast potatoes. For after forty years of married life what really was there left to say, except I still love you. *Tick....Tock....Grandfather....Clock.*

Occasionally he thought about beginnings, about how fate had brought him to the very place where he now sat. Beginnings of primary school, all excitement and fear; beginnings of secondary school and new friendships; courtship; marriage; career and parenthood. His wife had committed her life to family, the school where she taught and the community within which she lived. As they both approached retirement they discussed new beginnings, new adventures to make up for their commitment to others and not to themselves. Perhaps there would be short cruises to the sun, a visit to her sister in New Zealand or relaxing long weekends in York, Harrogate, Bath and elsewhere. But there would be no new beginnings for her, just the shock, the pain and the injustice of it all when she fell ill on the threshold of a dream.

After that there were very few beginnings for the old man, only endings. His wife long departed, friends funerals to attend and the marriages of both their daughters had not endured. Eighty five years? There must have been something more to it than this?

It was Wednesday and Mrs Simpson would not be here today. He picked up the paper and began to read the headlines. *Tick......Tick....* The change in the tone of the grandfather clock immediately attracted his attention for his antique George Parker had never ever let him down before? Oh dear, yet another ending he thought and carried on reading.

Mrs Simpson came punctually the following day and her duster, polish, dustpan and brush soon made their busy way from room to room. 'Mr A, you'll never guess who I saw in the post office today?' for that is what she affectionately called him. She was always Mrs S and he was always Mr A. But of course he would have guessed. He sat upright and silent in his armchair, his lifeless eyes gazing unseeing to the far horizon. *Tick......Tick....* If nothing else they always said goodbye and when she failed to hear his, 'Goodbye Mrs S', she would know that there would have to be new beginnings. *Tick....Tock....Grandfather....Clock.*

Trevor Cree
2022

Chapter 4
Bigbury Bay & Burgh Island

Thursday, 17th March 2022

One advantage of being based in a single location for an extended period of time is that you can pick and choose your days to go out and explore. That means that you can give the dull and rainy days a miss whilst also giving the busy weekends a wide berth, even though in March it is still relatively quiet in South Devon.

The weather forecast for Thursday was encouraging and so I decided that I would take Rucio to Bigbury Bay and Burgh Island. After topping up with petrol in California Cross at an exorbitant £1.85 per litre I was on my way, hoping as ever that Rucio would not let me down and leave me stranded in some remote location. She had never done so before but there was always a first time. On the road to Bigbury a well tended pond with a dry stone wall suddenly caught my eye and I just had to stop to take a photo before once again carrying on to my destination.

Dry stone wall and pond.

The actual village of Bigbury itself is some distance from the sea and so onwards it was to Bigbury-on-Sea and Burgh Island. Burgh Island is a small privately owned island that is accessible by foot at low tide whilst access is also possible by a specialist self-propelled people transporter on stilts (sea tractor) at high tide. That is probably more exciting than walking but clearly comes at a cost. The island is very limited in extent and the only buildings are the Pilchard Inn pub, the art deco Burgh Island Hotel and three private houses.

Burgh Island has past associations with Agatha Christie, Noel Coward and some television plays, such as Perrot and Lovejoy. In 2003 the new owners of the island erected signs closing all footpaths to the public but fortunately that decision was overturned in 2006. However in 2018 the island was again sold, this time to venture capitalists, and so goodness knows what they have in mind for the future but no doubt it won't involve you or me.

Every peak has to be climbed and so up I went the couple of hundred feet to a summit that afforded very good panoramic views of the rugged Devon coastline from east to west.

On such a fine day it was certainly worth the effort and after remaining a short time I chose a well grassed pathway to make my descent. I was carrying my crash helmet because, even after four years of ownership, I had still not worked out how to lock the luggage 'bike rack' onto the moped. I also happened to be wearing my ordinary smooth soled shoes and so the inevitable happened. Namely, I slipped on my back and let go of the helmet which immediately started to roll down the path.

The summit of Burgh Island.

I was concerned that my crash helmet would not only be damaged but that it might injure someone further down the slope. Chasing just behind it I managed to slip over once again whilst the helmet kept the same tantalising distance in front of me. Finally I managed to divert it off the path into some rougher ground where thankfully it finally came to a rest. It was a bit like a Charlie Chaplin movie but I was the reluctant star of the comedy. Fortunately when I looked around I don't think that anybody had seen my performance and so I proceeded to the bottom of the hill with only my muddy jeans as evidence that something untoward had happened. I was thankful that it had not been so much worse.

I put my head into the Pilchard Inn but understandably it was very busy and so I decided to recross the causeway on foot and head to a cafe that I had noticed high up in Bigbury-on-Sea. The view from the cafe was absolutely perfect and being on a very strict budget I restricted myself to a cup of coffee but then immediately gave way and had a slice of Victoria Sponge. This strict budget business is very difficult because place me within one hundred yards of a welcoming pub with a waft of hops and I cannot resist going inside for a single pint of local ale. For research purposes only of course.

Afternoon tea overlooking Burgh Island at low tide.

And talking of pubs, on my way to Bigbury-on-Sea I was passing through St Ann's Chapel and I had fleetingly seen a signpost to the

Journeys End pub. With a name like that it was impossible to resist making a visit. The pub is located in the small village of Ringmore and like so many other places in Devon it is difficult for cars to find somewhere to park. For those in the know there are actually a small number of parking spaces in the centre of the village but for Rucio and I we could park right outside the pub itself without obstructing access.

The Journeys End, Ringmore.

On entering the Journeys End I was very pleasantly surprised because quite a few people were having lunch and it is a wonderful ancient pub that still served beer from the barrel. Perhaps I should not drink beer when riding my moped or restrict myself to half a pint? Showing no such necessary discipline I therefore ordered a pint of 'Neep Tide' from the South Hams brewery. The Journeys End pub is a real gem and chance had certainly brought me to the right place. And then it was back to my 'home in the country' near Modbury for a power nap and whatever my journey to Noss Mayo the following day had in stall for me. Once again there would be one or two hiccups.

The Journeys End Pub.

Chapter 5
Circle

It was coming to the end of the class and the only item that Mr McCartan, the English language teacher, had to finalise was to set the subject for the coming weeks essay. Mr McCartan originally hailed from Northern Ireland, Newtownards to be precise, and he had brought with him to England his unique Ulster accent.

'Well the subject of this weeks essay, no more than 1,000 words as usual, is 'Circle'. And the essay is to be completed by next Wednesday. So it is.'

The class groaned.

The Northern Irish have an interesting habit of emphasising what they have just said with the phrase, 'So it is', as if the recipient might not have fully understood the first time. Even though it is unusual it is very pleasant to the ear. So it is.

Blenkinsop, the class swot, raised his chubby hand until he had caught Mr McCartan's eye
.
'Yes Blenkinsop?'

Chubby, for that was his predictable class nickname, peered over his half-moon glasses thereby giving an accurate impression of a well known politician at his most officious and asked.

'By circle Sir, do you mean a round plane figure whose boundary consists of points equidistant from a fixed point, or do you mean, a group of 'fwends' with shared interests?'

The class started giggling as they always did when Blenkinsop had trouble with his 'r's' because of his speech impediment.

'Quiet class, I'll have no more of that', said Mr McCartan. 'I've told you all before! Excellent point Blenkinsop', continued Mr McCartan. 'Whichever definition anyone chooses is the answer.'

Blenkinsop then sat back in his chair with a self-satisfied look on his face.

In the corner, at the very back of the class, Rowbotham was engrossed in his school iPad, set on mute, watching the YouTube video highlights of his team Liverpool against Everton. Salah had just curled the winner into the top righthand corner. Rowbotham's smart phone had been deposited, just like every other pupil, in a secure locker until the end of the school day. The school WiFi was not enabled for this particular classroom but his own mini router in his pocket solved that little problem.

'Rowbotham!', Mr McCartan said in a raised voice, 'Did you hear what I just said?'

'Yes Sir, our essay has to be in by next Wednesday, 1,000 words and no more. I was just writing it down on my iPad, Sir.'

'Thank you Mr Rowbotham. It is good to see that you are on the same planet for a change.'

Mr McCartan left the classroom and the noise rose by a number of decibels, for it was time to go home.

The following Wednesday came and the class rose as Mr McCartan entered the room. Well they were supposed to stand as a mark of respect for their teachers but as usual only Blenkinsop did so.

'Sit', said Mr McCartan, ignoring the fact that any such instruction was superfluous. 'Now class, have you all finished your essays?'

'Yes Sir', came the thoroughly disinterested response in unison.

'Now Mr Blenkinsop. I want you to write on the whiteboard the two definitions for 'Circle' that you identified last week.'

Blenkinsop rose and proceeded to write in large deliberate letters:
'CIRCLE'

- a round plane figure whose boundary consists of points equidistant from a fixed point.

- a group of friends with shared interests.

'Thank you Blenkinsop. You can return to your seat. Now of course the word 'Circle', with regard to the second definition, does not necessarily have to be a circle of friends but they may simply be people with a shared interest or profession. I will read out my marks at the end of each submission. Now who wants to read their essay first. Williams? Right off you go.'

At the back of the room Rowbotham's eyes widened and his complexion took on a paler hue. 'Circle?' 'Circle?' he mouthed without any sound being heard. I thought that Mac said 'Circus!' I'm certain he said 'Circus' but I was still watching the match at the time.

Rowbotham was immediately reminded of when his parents, his brother and himself were in Ulster for a holiday and they were staying at a small B & B in the country. At breakfast there was a grand display of the typical Ulster fry and he loved everything apart from the soda bread that he carefully left on the side of his plate. At the same table as the family a middle aged lady sat and the conversation turned to what everyone was planning to do that day. In her broad Ulster accent the lady said that she was going to Lisburn for the Service to which his younger brother enthusiastically responded.

'So you're going to the circus then? That sounds fun.'

His parents were embarrassed but the lady took it all in good heart and said 'No, I'm going to the Service. I'm a methodist minister.' Rowbotham just could not help laughing at his younger brother's mistake until the look that he received from his father soon brought him back into line.

And now fate had landed him in exactly the same embarrassing predicament. It was some sort of divine revenge he was sure.

Usually Rowbotham was bored to tears with the subject given for the essay but this time 'Circus' was a real surprise and he felt that even he could be enthused about it. He had never been to a circus in his life because they all seemed to be so boring, now that the wild animals had been removed from the act and all of the tightrope walkers had to wear safety harnesses, as did the bareback horse riders. There didn't seem to be much point going if someone didn't get maimed or gored.

Last year his parents took his brother and himself to Rome for a short educational holiday but it was all very boring with so many derelict ruins clearly in need of urgent repair. However what he did enjoy was the Circus Maximus where chariot racing took place in the old days and there were supposedly loads of crashes. Even better was the Colosseum where the English language audio guide described how gladiators used to fight each to the death, providing the Emperor turned his thumb down. He could just imagine himself as Emperor and he would never have put his thumb up, just down. The power of life over death was exhilarating as he pictured Blenkinsop looking up at him begging for his life. Thumbs down every time. And then there were the starving wild animals and the captured soldiers with no way to defend themselves but their bare hands. And they even flooded the place so that on really special occasions they could stage sea battles, once more to the death. Rowbotham had assumed that the same type of circus was staged in his own country many many years ago before everything had gone so soft. After all the Romans had been here, or so he had been told.

And so when Mr McCartan set 'Circus' as the subject for the essay Rowbotham was absolutely thrilled because this was a subject that he could actually write about and enjoy. The biggest problem that he faced was restricting his essay to less than 1,000 words because he had limbs flying everywhere, tightrope walkers falling into crocodile infested waters and so on. For the first time ever he was really looking forward to reading out his own essay. This time he would show them.

But now he just sat there in shock as one by one the class read out their pieces to a mixed reception. And then it was his turn.

'Ah, Rowbotham. Last but not least. What little gem of prose do you have for us this time?' asked Mr McCartan, with no little irony. The class sniggered. 'Come on Mr Rowbotham, let us all hear your piece and then we can all go home.'

Rowbotham hesitated. He could not possibly read out his 'Circus' essay full of gore and mayhem.

'Um. The area of a circle is 'pi' times the radius squared.' And that was it.

'Very good indeed Rowbotham. And?'

'Um. The tent of a circus is constructed in a circle, as is the circus ring itself' Again he hesitated.

'Very good Rowbotham. You are certainly excelling today compared to your previous efforts. And?', said Mr McCartan again waiting for further lines.

Rowbotham just sat there. Speechless.

Mr McCartan was a very patient man, as indeed all teachers have to be if they are to survive. But clearly that was it and so he walked over to look at Rowbotham's iPad to confirm for himself that Rowbotham's essay consisted of the sum total of just twenty seven words. Certainly better than previous Rowbotham efforts but what on earth could we do with this boy. He took Rowbotham's iPad from his hands and read out the title, 'Circus'.

The class laughed out loud as if of one voice. 'Circus!' they cried. 'Circus!' Rowey's really done it this time.

Mr McCartan studied the writing for a while and then read on so that all the class could hear. Limbs were certainly flying everywhere, battles were enjoined, lions were fed and the Emperor's thumb never turned to the sky. The words flowed until finally the bloody end was reached.

There was silence in the room. It was as if they had all had been transported back to a far gone age. It was so real.

Mr McCartan looked sternly at Rowbotham.

'Mr Rowbotham, you were clearly instructed to write an essay on the subject 'Circle' and what do we get, an essay entitled, 'Circus'. Zero marks for accuracy Mr Rowbotham. However. However Mr Rowbotham the writing was actually very good, the subject engrossing and even the grammar was more than acceptable. I'm therefore going to give you 9 out of 10 for content Mr Rowbotham. Well done.'

Rowbotham was amazed. The class were amazed. That is apart from Blenkinsop who had achieved the previous highest mark of 8. Blenkinsop glowered at Rowbotham and to make matters worse all of the class were by now gathered around Rowey to find our more about the Circus before they went home.

Trevor Cree
2022

Chapter 6
Stoke Bay & Noss Mayo

Friday, 18th March 2022

In comparison to yesterdays debacle of chasing a runaway crash helmet down a steep slope my planned visit to Noss Mayo looked to be much more straightforward. As the saying goes 'What could possibly go wrong?'

I had not checked the tyre pressures on Rucio for some time and so a visit to the petrol station at nearby California Cross seemed to be in order before I set off on what would be quite a long journey. I had previously noted that the petrol station had a coin operated air compressor that seemed to be exactly what I was looking for. Simply place the required coins in the slot, adjust the pressure setting, inflate the tyres and away you go. Simple.

In the 'old days' the pressure gauge was close to the valve connection point and you simply fed in air until the desired pressure had been reached and then disconnected. I had never had much success with the newer systems and so it turned out yet again. Rather than inflating the front tyre I managed to let all of the air out. I was a thirty minute walk from my campsite with an inoperable moped. A young man, who was helping out at the petrol station, could not have been more helpful and he came over to solve what was obviously a straightforward problem. Soon I would be on my way to Noss Mayo.

Unfortunately even he could not inflate the tyre and the only option remaining seemed to be for me to walk back to the campsite, drive Rocinante to California Cross, and take Rucio back to the campsite with my trip to Noss Mayo cancelled for the day. However the young man said that he would ask the cashier if she had a pump of some kind and indeed she thought that she might. And in her car was a very old foot pump with a pressure gauge attached and within a few minutes my front tyre was fully inflated and I was on my way. And how grateful I am to the young man and cashier who gave such 'old fashioned' service. Thanks to them both. Many many thanks.

View towards Bigbury Bay.

Technology and design are wonderful things but sometimes the simplest solutions still remain the best. The foot pump did not require a battery or electricity or a computerised pressure setting or a genius to operate it. I don't know how many times I have tried to enter hotel rooms around the world after a twelve hour flight and have taken an age to work out how to do so, often without success. And then it is back down with my baggage to the back of a lengthy queue at the check-in desk where the equivalent of Mr Bean is there to greet you, once again.

'How can I help you Sir?'

'My electronic key doesn't seem to work?'

'Ah, just let me see Sir?.....Yes, you are quite right. It seems that someone has given you the incorrect key for your room.'

'It was you who gave me the key.'

'Exactly so Sir. Here is your new key and your room is on the fifteenth floor.'
'
I know that it is on the fifteenth floor because I have just come from there.'

'Indeed Sir. We hope that you will enjoy your stay at the Cosmopolitan Grand.'

The wonderful film 'Trains, Planes & Automobiles' comes to mind. And with relief the door to your hotel room finally opens.

How to switch the lights on and more importantly how to switch them off? How to operate the wash basin and shower when there are no obvious clues how to do so? And hotel televisions have always been beyond my capabilities. It is often like a proficiency test that must be passed. But I digress.

According to my detailed map the scenic coastal route to Noss Mayo would take me via Holbeton, Mothecombe, Battisborough Cross, Stoke Bay and finally on to my destination, Noss Mayo. However to reach Holbeton I would have to pass through Modbury and join the A379 in order to cross the River Erme. Main road traffic and mopeds speeding along at a breathtaking 25 mph do not really mix. I was therefore greatly relieved, as no doubt were they, when the minor road turnoff to Holbeton was finally reached.

I did not actually stop in Holbeton but a pub did not escape my notice for a future visit. It seems that the village actually has two, the 'Mildmay

Colours' and the 'Dartmoor Union'. Mothecombe is located close to the mouth of the River Erme and from there I had hoped to follow what I thought was a very minor road along the actual coastline. There is ample parking and a cafe just beyond the village but since I had far to go I continued down the lane to the estuary itself where my intended route unfortunately came to a dead end. My anticipated lane along the coastline was in fact the South West Coast Path and so it was back to Plan B, even though I did not have a Plan B.

It soon became apparent that I had to first go to Battisborough Cross and only then would I be able to follow a lane parallel to the coastline all of the way to Noss Mayo. I had not studied the route in detail but chance is often the best way to find sites of particular interest. Bowling along narrow Devon lanes is always an interesting experience and clearly they were not built for the motorcar but for the much quieter and slower age of the pedestrian, horse rider, cart and possibly carriage.

The car is out of its natural environment and I imagine that in peak season the intended restful and relaxing summer holiday for the family quickly turns into a stressful competition about who has the right of way and who should back up. Overall I believe, apart from London, that British drivers are very considerate with a waved acknowledgement for every good deed. But not so on Devon lanes in summer I fear. And so it was with undisguised smugness that Rucio and I made our way further west, occasionally giving way to an impatient Mr Toad who was clearly in haste to get somewhere or other very fast.

It was a clear blue sky day, even if a little chill, but soon views of the rugged coastline and sparkling sea presented themselves through breaks in the high hedgerows. Further along Mr Toad's house came into view with the most lopsided chimney that I have ever seen. The bushes and trees are characteristically bowed to the prevailing wind in this area but I have never seen a chimney influenced to the same degree. Clearly it wasn't but how it has not collapsed into rubble on the ground before now is a secret known only to the owner. It was indeed a house fitting for Mr Toad of Toad Hall and well worth a return visit in the future.

Shortly afterwards I encountered the bane of every commuters life, the traffic jam. There was no warning except that a farm worker on a trail bike passed me in the opposite direction and very soon after I came across another farm worker on a quad bike who was blocking a lane that headed north. It was clear that something was up and so I asked the man on the quad bike and he suggested that I pull into the side of the lane because some cattle would soon be passing by. And when they came it was like a Union Pacific freight train that kept coming and coming as if the wagons would never end. The young calves, for that was what they were, in general ignored me but the more inquisitive ones came for a closer look. And finally they were past and at the end of the line another man on a quad bike was riding shotgun and as he passed I shouted 'How many?' to which he replied 'Two hundred' and then he was gone.

Toad Hall

Further along the lane an indistinct sign informed me that to the left could be found an 'historic church' and since it had to be located close to the sea I went to further investigate. Revelstoke Park is primarily a site for park homes but public access is granted to two scenic sites not to be missed, namely Stoke Bay and the church ruin of 'St Peter the Poor

Fisherman'. There is parking space available for approximately twelve cars and little alternative on the access road where various signs make it quite clear that parking is not permitted. Because of the parking limitations it is unlikely that Stoke Bay beach is ever teeming with bathers and indeed, although there is plenty of sand, it is the gigantic rocks that make the greatest impression.

St Peter the Poor Fisherman.

St Peter the Poor Fisherman is one of those churches that would probably no longer exist if it were not for the Churches Conservation Trust. In my travels to my randomly selected locations throughout England, Wales and Scotland I have by chance seen a number of similarly preserved churches and each is uniquely special. St Peter the Poor Fisherman, although only partially roofed, remains open for occasional services and events. The first documented record of the church is 1225 although the experts say that it may date back to the 10th century Anglo Saxon period based on the fabric of the church itself. It was a long climb back up to where Rucio patiently waited for me but well worth the time and effort.

As I drew closer to Noss Mayo I took a small diversion to Worswell in the hope of finding some fine coastal views. Although there was a National Trust car park I did not take the time to walk the short distance to the South West Coast Path where I assume that the views must have been. Higher priorities beckoned, namely a pub stop in Noss Mayo.

St Peter the Poor Fisherman.

Apparently there are two pubs in Noss Mayo, the 'Ship Inn' and the 'Swan Inn', but it was the former that I came across first. The pub was visible from a small car park where, since it was low tide, cars were happily parked on the firm sand below the clearly designated high water mark. 'Now where did I leave the car last night Janice when we had too many to drive home? I'm sure I will remember soon.' The Ship Inn has an extensive patio seating area overlooking the small inlet on which the pub is located. It was a perfect day to have something to eat and drink and so financial self-discipline went straight out of the window once again. I had a pint from the Noss Mayo brewery and could not resist the scallops, bacon, new potatoes and salad. After all, I logically reasoned, fish and chips was fifteen pounds and since the scallops were only two pounds more at seventeen pounds then it was an absolute bargain.

Scallops, The Ship Inn, Noss Mayo.

After a very relaxed hour it was time to retrace my steps and return home. I could have taken a different route of country lanes but sometimes returning in the exact opposite direction provides a completely different perspective and indeed different views. On such a beautiful day it was the right decision and as always return journeys seem so much shorter, although perhaps that could have been the pint of beer.

Although none was forecast I put the rain cover on Rucio after my arrival home because the wind was starting to gust strongly and weather forecasts can sometimes be magnificently wrong. The next morning, before I was fully awake, I looked out of the window to see that Rucio was lying on her side on the ground. Apparently lifeless! My first thought was that it must be Potomac horse fever until I cleverly deduced that Rucio was a moped and not a donkey. The wind had certainly been very severe during the night but I had not heard a thing, no crashing, no dull thump.

How amazingly stupid I had been putting the rain cover on when it would clearly act as a large sail whereas without the cover the wind would simply have whistled through the frame. I gently lifted Rucio up expecting the very worst, broken handlebars, damaged fuel tank, twisted forks and so on. But no, the only damage was a dislodged and loose wing mirror and a luggage pannier fixing that had broken, both relatively easy for me to fix. Without Rucio my life would have had to change dramatically and I didn't fancy the option of cycling up and down the steep Devon hills on a bicycle. The nearest bus stop is located two miles away from my home and so that would not have been a feasible option. However a short test drive the very same day demonstrated that Rucio was made of much sterner stuff than I imagined and all was indeed well. The next visit with Rucio was to be to Kingsbridge, to tilt at more windmills, but that is another story

Chapter 7
Wildlife

My home is on the edge of the wild wood. It was where I was born and it is where my ancestors have lived for as long as can be remembered.

Each morning I wake up just before dawn and in late May, as it is now and when conditions are conducive, I preen myself in the warmth of a sun that rises far to the east. Although it may be immodest for me to say I am a fine looking specimen, as indeed are all of our kind. My pale underside is speckled with black dots, like coals in recently fallen snow. My beautiful tail extends in a wide fan and the outer tips are black thereby accentuating its size and form. My overcoat is of chestnut brown whilst my head is grey giving the impression of age. But I am not old.

My land stretches as far as the eye can see over open fields right up to the ridge line on the horizon. I never venture deep into the wild wood for that is not my territory nor are my particular skills best suited to that environment. The hedgerows and fields are where I prefer to be and each day that is where the food for my small growing family is to be found.

Stretching my wings to full extent I dive down from my high perch in the oak tree and rapidly gaining speed I then rise into the still air until I am one hundred feet or more above the ground. I hover for a while, looking, searching, waiting. My eyesight is so sharp that I can even see a beetle from this height although my main quarry is field mouse and vole. That is my preference but sometimes at this time of year I do not turn down the very young rabbits that are far too easy to catch with their bobbing tails of white. If fortune is not favourable in one location I speedily move on to another and then to another where I hover precisely where I am. Then diving down I swoop on an unsuspecting victim and grasp the same in my yellow talons so tight that none can escape. And then without delay it is back to our oak tree where the family awaits. I leave almost immediately for my partner can well look after herself and our young ones, and all need to be fed.

About midday, when the sun is at its highest, my work for the day is about done. Mostly I rest in the shade of the tree but sometimes I grow impatient and decide to explore beyond the ridge line that marks the limit of my territory. For in the next valley 'The Others' live.

'The Others' are far different from us in every way. They do not live in the trees, hedgerows or burrows in the ground but in structures more reminiscent of the beehives that they like to keep. I find their lives just as fascinating as I find them incomprehensible. Sometimes I hover high above but usually I select a telegraph pole or sit on the wires so that I may more easily observe their strange behaviour. Usually they do not look up and so I can observe them unseen but when, on occasion, they do it is not in an unfriendly way. However if I sense any threat I am far away before they have time to think of the next thought that is about to enter their head.

The beehives that they build were traditionally of natural wood, earth and thatch but now they are invariably of brick, clay tile and stone. Each day they appear out of the same hole in the wall as if in a rush to get somewhere else very quickly. Sometimes they walk at pace, sometimes they enter a vehicle that speeds down the highway and around a distant corner out of sight. Wherever they are going and whatever they are going to do must be very important for it seems that they have little time to speak to their fellow 'Others'. My eyesight and hearing are acute and I can read their lips or hear them say, 'Sorry Marge, must dash, I have an appointment at so and so.' I never see them out hunting and so I have no idea how they survive, but somehow they do. The fields of Devon are a paradise for natural grass and corn but I never see them grazing. It is all very strange.

I do however see them go into beehives, usually the female 'Others', where nobody lives. On their later appearance they are usually carrying something or other with a contented appearance on their faces. Into and out of various beehives they go reminding me of bees skipping from one flower to another harvesting nectar. And when they are fully laden I follow them back to their own beehives, through the hole in the wall they go, never to be seen again that day. Later the male 'Other' returns on foot or rapidly comes to a halt in their vehicle with a look of impatience and frustration on their faces. Similarly they pace at speed through the hole in the wall.

The 'Others' are a fascinating species but I will never understand them or how they survive. After a while, with a feeling of gratitude for my own life, I return to my home and family on the edge of the wild wood where everything makes perfect sense.

Trevor Cree 2022

Chapter 8
Kingsbridge

<u>Wednesday, 23rd March 2022</u>

Originally I had thought that I might take the 'stretch limo' (bus) from Modbury to Kingsbridge but since it was only five miles away I decided to give Rucio another outing. I did not anticipate any untoward incidents occurring this time but with my recent run of luck anything could happen. Firstly I headed back towards California Cross and then south along the B3196 towards Loddiswell. On the approach to the village there were road signs that warned articulated vehicles that they should not proceed any further and that they were required to take an alternative route. The roads of Loddiswell were not as narrow as I had therefore expected nor the corners quite as tight but it was clear that past events had required the warning signs to be put in place.

The Loddiswell Inn flashed by unvisited and then it was down to the New Bridge crossing of the River Avon, which predictably was actually very old and Grade II listed. And then on to Kingsbridge itself with the first priority being to find a car park with free parking for Rucio. The Lower Union Road car park was ideal and after I had assured myself that I would not receive a parking ticket this time, as I had in Lyme Regis, I made my way to the Town Square which is located right at the head of the Kingsbridge estuary itself.

As the crow flies Kingsbridge is approximately five miles from the sea but it does not seem that far because just south of the town the estuary widens out significantly only to narrow once again closer to Salcombe. It was high tide and the estuary therefore looked at its very best and so I decided to walk south along the eastern side of the waters edge towards the Crabshell Inn and possibly beyond.

We will remember them.

A memorial to the men of Kingsbridge and Dodbridge, who lost their lives in what is described as the 'Great War 1914-1918', sits close to the water and at the base a multitude of pebbles from the seashore had been placed. One pebble in particular caught my eye and on it were the handwritten words 'We will remember them, 2nd Kingsbridge Brownies'. After more than one hundred years it is good to see that their sacrifice is still recognised, even by the very young.

Old mooring post, Kingsbridge.

As the estuary started to broaden the view back towards town became particularly beautiful whilst the smooth pathway encouraged, even implored, one to walk further. Even though new waterside apartments had been built in recent years it was clear that the original public footpath, directly next to the waters edge, had been retained, however much the developers would have liked to have denied access for the exclusive benefit of their clients. The phrase 'absolutely waters edge' had been a major selling point of beachfront properties in New Zealand when I lived there but after the recent tsunamis in other parts of the world it is unlikely that those words retain quite the same attraction today. The Crabshell Inn was soon reached and although I was expecting a typical old English pub it was actually quite modern. It was too early in the day for a pint and so I sat down at a wooden table and had a coffee and a triple chocolate muffin instead.

It was yet another glorious day to just sit and relax exactly where I was but Britton's Field in the distance beckoned and it seemed from my map to offer extensive views of the estuary. More apartments, this time built right on the water, required a small diversion from the path to Embankment Road. Large black wrought iron security gates caught my eye with an adjacent magnolia in full bloom. 'Fear of strangers' is a recurrent theme today but we have lived with this fear ever since the first prehistoric hill forts were constructed thousands of years ago and nothing has really changed.

Britton's Field, Kingsbridge.

The route continued to follow Embankment Road for a short distance and then the Britton's Field picnic site finally came into view. It was most certainly worth the effort because it did indeed provide a panoramic view of the sparkling waters all the way down towards Salcombe, that must have been hidden from view just around a distant bend. At low tide perhaps the view of extensive mud flats might not be so impressive to most of us although the most enthusiastic bird watchers would no doubt strongly disagree.

My attention was then caught by a 'finger post' sign informing me that I was actually on the 'Waterside Walk' and it pointed me back towards the town centre. Apart from the distance of three-quarters of a mile and an approximate walking time of 15 minutes what was particularly bizarre, at least to my mind, was that it also stated that I would require 65 calories in order to complete the journey. Not 64 calories nor 66 calories but a very precise 65. Did I have 65 calories remaining in the tank I asked myself? Would I simply expire within touching distance of the town centre?

Finger post.

Smart phones have their uses and a quick check informed me that a rich tea biscuit, one oatcake or a medium orange each contained fifty calories. But on checking my pockets I had none of those life saving items. But then I remembered the large triple chocolate muffin that I had eaten just a short time before and after checking my smart phone again it appears that each muffin contains approximately 500 calories. Not only could I risk the walk back to town but it appeared that I was in danger of becoming decidedly obese.

Back at the Crabshell Inn I noticed a splendid 'room with a view' that was clearly once 'The Old Boathouse' but is now a private residence with a very picturesque balcony to relax on and look down on lesser mortals, such as myself.

Before too long I was once again back in the Town Square and at the information office I obtained a map of the town, guides to some recommended walks and beaches in the area and some greeting cards. Fore Street is clearly the shopping heart of old Kingsbridge and the road itself rises very steeply towards Stentiford Hill. I have now come across three streets named Fore Street in South Devon, one here in Kingsbridge, one in Salcombe and one in Aveton Gifford. Clearly the widely accepted claim that Scotland was the origin of the game of golf is simply a myth because the South Devon area must now take that title with everyone in the surrounding villages shouting 'Fore!' when playing golf in the dirt road. It is just that they were clearly not very good at it.

Chapter 9
The Colour of Money

Just before 8.30 a.m. every weekday I enter the Lloyds Bank branch in Fore Street in order to prepare for opening at 9.00 a.m. I have worked at the branch for nearly 40 years and during that time I have observed many changes that my younger colleagues will not have witnessed. The main change being that fewer and fewer customers visit our branch and they are in the main, like myself, of the older generation. We have three counters in the Fore Street branch and my counter deals with 'Special Transactions' that take longer to deal with and therefore the queue is likewise longer. The doors open and here they come now, familiar faces from over the years.

'Good morning Lady Macmillan. How can I help you today?'

'Ah, good morning Mrs Cooper. What fine weather we are having just lately. And how is Mr Cooper? I don't seem to see much of anybody nowadays since Harold passed away.'

'Mr Cooper is well thank you Your Ladyship. Many thanks for asking. And how can I help you?'

'Well I was searching through Harold's bureau the other day and I found a cheque for 32 pounds 5 shillings and 5 pence made out in my name. I wonder if I could deposit it in my savings account please?'

'I see that it is dated the 5th April 1953 Lady Macmillan. I don't see many cheques nowadays and especially such beautiful ones as this. Your husband had such wonderful handwriting didn't he. Here is your receipt. Can I be of further assistance Your Ladyship?'

'No, thank you very much Mrs Cooper. You have indeed been very helpful. It is so reassuring being able to speak to someone in person. Good day.'

'Good Morning Earl Russell. How can I help you today?'

'Good morning Mrs Cooper. I should like to deposit these coins and notes into my current account thank you. I have double checked the amount. It comes to 125 pounds and 9 shillings and 6 pence. You will find a few farthings, ha'pennies, half crowns, florins and so on but the majority are actually one pound notes.'

'Thank you Mr Russell. If you would be so kind as to to wait for a few moments I will check the amount and give you your receipt. I must admit that I did enjoy the third volume of your autobiography.'

'Well thank you Mrs Cooper.'

And with that I tipped the multitude of coins and notes onto the counter, separated them into small piles of the same denomination, counted them carefully and deposited the proceeds into individual brown paper envelopes with the exact amount written on each.

'Exactly so Mr Russell. A total of 125 pounds and 9 shillings and 6 pence. Here is your receipt. Can I be of any further assistance?'

'No thank you Mrs Cooper. You have been very helpful as usual. Good day.'

'Good morning Mr Johnson. How can I help you today?'

'Good morning Mrs Cooper. I should like to deposit these gold sovereigns into my account.'

'That is no problem Mr Johnson. I'll just check the amount and conversion rate and provide you with a receipt. And how is your dictionary of the English language coming on?'

'Very well thank you Mrs Cooper. I had hoped to finish it within three years but it has so far taken eight. Never mind, it is now finally at the printers. I believe that it will make a significant contribution to our nation.'

'There you are Mr Johnson, a receipt for 205 pounds and 50 pence.'

'Thank you very much Mrs Cooper. Good day to you.'

'Good morning Mr Qln. How can I help you today?'

'Good morning Mrs Cooper. I should like to deposit these bronze coins into my account. I am not exactly sure of their current value but I know that you will have the necessary valuation for today.'

'Thank you Mr Qin. I shall just have to check on the computer. And how is Lady Fu Hao today? In good health I hope?'

'Indeed she is Mrs Cooper. I am sure that she will reign over our Shang nation for many years to come.'

'That is so reassuring to hear Mr Qin. The current exchange rate is 1 Shang bronze coin equals 10.5563 English pounds. And so the 300 coins that you wish to deposit comes to £3,166.89, less £47.50 transaction fee, giving a net total £3,119.39.'

'That sounds excellent Mrs Cooper. I trust you implicitly.'

'Then here is your receipt Mr Qin. Good day.'

'Good morning Mr Hammurabi. How can I help you today?'

'Good morning Mrs Cooper. I should like to deposit these five lambs and two hens in exchange for some hand tools and wood please.'

'That should be fine Mr Hammurabi. I will just close my counter and meet you in the Special Transaction room as usual.'

'Thank you Mrs Cooper.'

'Now Mr Hammurabi. We will just have to weigh the lambs and hens in order to get an equivalent value. Head office says that we can no longer simply barter like we used to do in the past.'

'Oh, that's a pity Mrs Cooper. It takes all the enjoyment away as far as I am concerned. Oh well, I guess that is what they call progress.'

'I have to agree with you Mr Hammurabi but orders are orders. Now if you would just like to look at the hand tools and wood that we have in stock. They are all marked in shekel equivalent.'

'Shekel equivalent! Whatever next. They will be making us buy and sell with shekels soon.'

'Probably not before I retire Mr Hammurabi. I see that you have brought your Umma slave to help you today.'

'Indeed I have. A rather surly fellow but strong. I should like to exchange my produce for a wood plane, hammer, chisel, wood drill and five standard lengths of oak, if I may Mrs Cooper.'

'I am afraid that you have only deposited enough goods for four standard lengths Mr Hammurabi. Would that be acceptable?'

'Oh well, I suppose that it will have to be Mrs Cooper. Shall we shake hands on that then?'

'Indeed Mr Hammurabi. As you know Lloyds Bank's word is its bond.'

And with that a contented Mr Hammurabi and his slave left the branch with their purchases and it was time to close the branch because it was already approaching 3.00 p.m. It was just another typical day in Kingsbridge and as I walked down the hill towards the bus station I considered myself so very fortunate to have such an interesting employment and customers. And with that I wondered who I would chance to meet tomorrow?

Trevor Cree
2022

Chapter 10
Bantham & Thurlestone

Wednesday, 20th April 2022

On the 20th April, my late mother's birthday, I woke to a clear blue sky. I knew immediately that the gods had decided that today was the very day that myself and Rucio would visit Bantham, Thurlestone and Hope Cove. I had never heard of those three locations before I arrived to live in Modbury for the summer. My cousin was the first to alert me to the attractions of Thurlestone since she and her husband had spent many happy holidays there with their young daughter and friends. In a similar vein another friend of mine mentioned that he and his wife had taken their own children camping in Bantham for a number of years. The third location, Hope Cove, came about by a chance encounter with a retired couple that I briefly met as they were leaving the California Inn in California Cross to go to their holiday home in Hope Cove. As chance would have it the three villages were all located within a short distance of each other providing me with the opportunity to kill three birds with one stone, if that is not an inappropriate expression.

Based on our past experience a significant objective for Rucio and myself was to avoid the main roads at all costs because mopeds and normal road traffic simply do not mix. This is particularly true with the recent introduction of the new Highway Code rules that state that when passing cyclists cars now have to leave a gap of three miles. Understandably car owners are not at all happy about it. I therefore studied my map in great detail and made a list of the locations that we would need to pass through whilst only using the lanes, namely Loddiswell, Churchstow, Upton and Buckland in order to get to the very first destination of Bantham. In addition to my handwritten notes I also had a very detailed 4 cm to 1 km Ordnance Survey map. What on earth could possibly go wrong after such meticulous planning?

The journey to Loddiswell and over the River Avon at New Bridge was absolutely fine because we had used that same route on the previous visit to Kingsbridge. However shortly after the bridge we sailed straight past the planned turning to Churchstow because, with true Devonian cunning, there was actually no signpost to Churchstow itself. We soon realised that we must have passed the turning and so we simply retraced our steps down a very steep hill at speed followed closely behind by an enormous tractor that I hoped would see our infinitely small indicator light frantically blinking left, left, left.

Once in the relative safety of the lane we stopped, retrieved my detailed map from my daypack and soon determined that we simply needed to take the next second left and that would take us directly to Churchstow. What could be easier. Now the slight difficulty with consulting my very detailed map is that it is absolutely huge being four feet by three feet in extent and all having to be carefully unfolded and refolded before and after use. Fortunately there was very little breeze on the day in question. Problem solved and we were on our way again just looking for the second turning left.

Within an unexpectedly short distance we came to the first turning left and there, bold as brass, was a signpost to Churchstow. Not as we thought the second turning left it is true but how could we possibly ignore an actual signpost to Churchstow when signposts in the lanes of South Devon are a rarity, or at least signposts with all directions fully intact. Left turn it was then. However what had previously been a very narrow lane quickly became a very very narrow lane but wonderful for all that. We soon came upon a very impressive building of ancient heritage towering above the lane, namely Leigh Barton.

Leigh Barton.

Rucio demanded that we stop and take a photograph, which I obediently did. Photograph duly taken it was then onwards and up a very steep tree lined hill. I had not read anything in the papers but it seems that there must be tigers in the vicinity because there, right in the middle of the lane, was a massive tiger trap. On reflection it may not have actually been a tiger trap but simply one of the largest potholes that I had ever seen. If, as we intended, we came back the same way we would have to take great care not to drive straight into it because otherwise there would not be a happy ending for either Rucio or I.

Finally we came to the top of the hill but not in Churchstow itself as intended but to Higher Leigh Farm and Leigh Cross that were located on another dreaded main road. And so once again it was out with the map, as large as a sail for rounding Cape Horn, to determine where we actually were in the world. All became perfectly clear. I had been cunningly deceived by the signpost and Churchstow itself was at least two miles to the west along the main road. However we quickly worked out that if we simply crossed over the main road another lane would take us in the direction of Upton and South Milton and therefore much closer to where we ultimately wanted to be, namely Bantham.

The lanes of South Devon.

There were lovely views from on high as we rode along, though ominously in close proximity to Kingsbridge where we certainly did not want to be. Finally our route brought us to yet another junction with once again no helpful signposts to be seen. When looking back towards where we had just come we saw a road sign with an exclamation mark stating 'IGNORE SAT NAV Congestion Narrow Lane'. I did not remember seeing a similar sign at the other end of the lane and so how many unsuspecting holidaymakers had been drawn to their fate and into the tiger trap by their Sat Nav I have no idea but certainly enough to justify the cost of the road sign. The impressive stone columned entrance to some mansion or other stood close by but it was only later that I learned that the estate was named 'Bowringsleigh' but since we did not have an invitation we simply carried on our way.

River Avon, Bantham.

Our error strewn outings may seem rather odd but it reminds me of when my mother and I would take random journeys in my car along the lanes of Sussex, It was simply a matter of taking a random left followed by a random right followed by random turns in each direction and also using our instincts about which way to go. The number of wonderful days we had with so many unexpected and beautiful discoveries. But time was rapidly passing and so on Rucio and I travelled through Heddeswell Cross to Upton Cross until at last we finally found an actual signpost to Buckland and Bantham.

Bantham is ideally located at the mouth of the River Avon and when the tide is in, which it was on that particular day, it is certainly a beautiful setting. The 'Sloop Inn' beckoned but it was still too early for opening and so we followed the road towards the sea until our route was blocked by a barrier and armed guards. Well not exactly because it was simply that to proceed further we would have had to pay two pounds for a motorcycle whilst cars have to pay over six pounds. A sign proclaimed that it was 'Private Property' and that 'No Lorries, No Coaches, No Camping, No Overnight Parking' and 'No Sex' were permitted. Well I exaggerate slightly about the sex part.

I do appreciate that we have to pay for parking in most places now and that there are real costs of upkeep for such special locations but we could not even see the beach from where we were. Since we still had to visit Thurlestone and Hope Cove that day I did not think that it was worth two of my precious pounds just to take a quick glimpse at a piece of sand.

As we were about to continue our journey I noticed, half hidden by a bush and barely legible, an inscription on a stone plaque inserted in a wall that read 'These seats were put here by the people of Bantham and Buckland 16-4-30'. And so the wooden seats, or perhaps their later replacements, are still in place after all these years for local people and visitors alike to enjoy a wonderful view of the River Avon. Free of any charge.

And so it was then on to Thurlestone and that required retracing our route for a short distance up the Buckland Stream and then on down into Thurlestone itself. On the side of the road, just before Thurlestone, I noticed a small pick-up truck parked with what seemed to be reeds for thatching in the back and so we stopped to investigate further. And there on the right was a dilapidated cottage, or at least the thatch was very dilapidated, with three men hard at work demonstrating their ancient skills. It was a wonderful and unexpected sight. After taking some photographs I said to one of the men standing on high 'There are not many of you left now, are there?' to which came the response 'Dozens'. This was most certainly a surprise, but a very pleasant one for all that.

The craft of thatching.

On arrival in Thurlestone itself we came quickly to a halt at the 'Village Inn' that most certainly looked inviting but with shear willpower onwards we went, past the Thurlestone Hotel, until we arrived at the clubhouse of the Thurlestone Golf Club. A sign helpfully informed all and sundry to 'BEWARE. Golf balls from the right. Please walk across quickly' thereby providing further indisputable proof of my theory that golf originated in South Devon but that they were, and are still not, very good at it. The golf course itself hugs the sea and on a fine day, like today, nothing could be better. However when a raging westerly blows in the winter I would imagine that the warmth of the clubhouse itself would be far too difficult to resist.

Thurlestone Golf Club.

Chapter 11
Joy!

A few days ago I decided to make an outing to Wonwell Beach and explore a mile or two of the South West Coast Path. It was a blue sky day and because the tide was still incoming the golden sands could be seen at their very best. The footpath was well graded and provided panoramic views far out to the west towards the approaches to Plymouth and beyond. The path was like a roller coaster following the rise and fall of the sheer cliffs that overlooked the clear waters below. For experienced walkers the route offered no real physical challenge and within a few hours they would have passed through Hope Cove, Bolberry Hill until finally they would have reached Salcombe itself. However for someone of my years the heat of the day was becoming oppressive and more importantly it was by now opening time at the Dolphin Inn, in nearby Kingston. The Siren voices called and drew me towards my fate, like the companions of Odysseus.

The Dolphin Inn is a fine rural pub in which to spend an hour or two relaxing in the shade of the trees with a pint of Jail Ale in your hand. I am not particularly proud of the fact but when I feel a bit weary after a strenuous walk and a pint or two I will sometimes go to the nearby church to undertake some 'historical research', or more accurately for a short nap. Usually the village churches that I visit are deserted during the working day. I head for the pews close to the front, but just to one side, and there I can sit undisturbed as if in devout worship with my hands clasped together on the pew in front, my forehead resting on my hands. My devotion usually lasts for about thirty minutes or so and providing I do not snore I am invariably left completely to myself.

I had had a wonderful slumber in 'St James the Less' and feeling much refreshed I sat up. To my great surprise a man was sitting just a few feet away from me and he had appeared so quietly that at first I thought that he was an apparition. He was smartly dressed in collar, jacket and tie which seemed inappropriate for a hot summers day but he showed no sign of the heat. I sat there in surprise because in the whole expanse of the church this man had decided to sit close to me. Like most people I value my personal space and this man had clearly intruded upon it but I was more intrigued than annoyed. We sat there in silence for a few minutes until the man finally spoke and asked me what my plans for the future were. I simply replied that I expected to remain in South Devon for the remainder of the summer after which I would be returning to my home in Sussex. The man then said 'Sorry, I did not make myself quite clear. I meant what are your plans for your death, for that is the only certainty in life?'

I was not at all shocked by such a question because this man had a kindly demeanour. The question made a pleasant change from the rather banal conversations that we tend to strike up when meeting someone for the very first time. However before I could answer the man handed me a menu, very similar in format to those one sees in high class restaurants, the words clearly outlined in beautiful flowing script. Rather than a list of mouthwatering delicacies divided into starters and mains this menu was a comprehensive list of all of the ways that it was possible to die.

I studied the menu with no more concern than I would looking at the menu in a restaurant. I had never previously considered that there were so many different ways to die before and it really was something of a revelation. The starters on the menu were non-fatal events such as mini-strokes, heart arrhythmia, early dementia and so on. Unpleasant in themselves but simply a taster of things to come. The extent of the mains was astounding. As the master of storytelling, travel writing and food critic A.A. Gill stated when describing his own personal diagnosis the 'Full English' of cancers was included. As I read on the man sat quietly and observed my reaction. He then spoke once more and said 'The choice is yours. As a man of faith the choice of your passing is within your own hands. I am giving you a choice that is denied to most.'

I felt that I must tell this saintly man that I was not actually a person of faith and that I had only visited the church because I needed somewhere to have a rest, but somehow it seemed far too late to do so. After all it's not every day that you find yourself conversing with someone who is offering you a gift beyond value. I simply enquired 'Why on earth should someone choose to die in a fire, or in a plane crash or similar? It does not make sense when so many other kinder deaths are possible.'

He pondered my question for a moment and then proceeded to explain as follows 'It's like choosing from a menu in an Indian restaurant. Most people will choose a korma, balti or dansak but there are those who always have to go for a vindaloo and always demand that it is extra hot. It's human nature really.'

I looked at the menu in detail once more and carefully appraised the multitude of options. Did I really want Alzheimer's? Bowel cancer? Was I really brave enough to choose one of the vindaloos? No, most certainly not. I was a coward when it came to the point and so I chose number 45, 'Passing away in your sleep.' I then handed back the menu and the man acknowledged my decision with the words 'It is done.'

I leant down for my daypack and there were so many further questions that I wanted to ask but when I looked up again the man had gone. Vanished in an instant. I metaphorically pinched myself to make sure but there was no doubt that what had happened was real. I had not just awakened from a dream. It was such a relief and all my concerns about death that I had never fully confronted before had been dispatched in an instant. I could live every day as if it were my last in the certain knowledge that when my end came I would know nothing about it. I called out loud 'Oh Joy! Oh Great Joy!' and the words echoed around the vaults and arches. No longer would I have to worry about the future and I suddenly experienced a feeling of overwhelming happiness.

It was by now time to return to my temporary home in the country and so I left the church after placing a generous twenty pound note in the collection box. The path from the church is rather steep but instead of taking the graded wheelchair pathway I decided to take the steps and tripping on one of the large flagstones I fell headlong into the stone wall by the gate. I hit my head with a mighty blow but what happened after that I have absolutely no recollection.

....

The Coroner's report in the South Hams Gazette precisely recorded the unfortunate death of a visitor to the area, namely Mr John Gilbody. The coroner stated that Mr Gilbody had visited the Dolphin Inn in the village prior to his making a visit to the adjacent church. Little was known about Mr Gilbody but he was clearly a spiritual man because he had been observed visiting a number of churches in the locality during the past few weeks, including All Hallows, Saint Peter the Poor Fisherman and All Saints, where he had been observed in deep prayer. The landlord of the Dolphin Inn reported that Mr Gilbody had quietly consumed two pints of ale before he left the premises at about 1.30 p.m. Based on that timing it would appear that Mr Gilbody had spent approximately one hour in quiet reflection but on leaving the church he had unfortunately tripped and fallen by the main gate and had suffered a fractured skull. A passer-by saw him stumble and fall but there was nothing that she could do apart from telephone for an ambulance. The last words that Mr Gilbody uttered before he succumbed were reported by the lady to have been 'That's not what I ordered off the menu' but by then he was somewhat delirious.

Cause of Death: Accidental'.

Trevor Cree
2022

Chapter 12
Hope Cove

<u>Wednesday, 20th April 2022 (cont'd)</u>

Further along the coast Hope Cove was said to be very scenic including a harbour and at least one pub and so we continued in that general direction. Bolberry Down, that lies just beyond Hope Cove, also looked to be well worth a visit with its location on sheer cliffs that rise high above the sea far below. And so instead of stopping in Outer Hope we carried on through Inner Hope with the intention of returning later for something to eat and drink.

Bolberry Down is most certainly worth a visit. It is a National Trust owned site where parking is free for members but a charge of two pounds is made for non-members. I was busily inspecting the noticeboard to see if there was a charge for motorcycles when a man in a car drove up wearing a National Trust top and he helpfully informed me that parking was free for Rucio whose fame must have preceded her. What better invitation did we need to make a longer stay at Bolberry Down and the pint of best would just have to wait.

Bolberry Down.

The jagged cliffs rise vertically from the sea at Bolberry Down whilst far below waves were breaking over the rock outcrops that lay in wait ready to welcome the unwary sailor. The views were certainly very impressive, particularly on another clear blue sky day like today. If visitors wish they can walk the South West Coast Path from there towards Hope Cove or in the opposite direction towards Salcombe. I chose the much easier option and did neither and so it was back to Outer Hope where we stopped for lunch.

The view from the heights above Inner Hope is outstandingly beautiful as is the little church that looks far out to sea. No doubt that sacred place has a very long history to tell of happiness, celebration, sadness and despair. A yacht lies at anchor in the bay below sitting on transparent waters of pale and dark blue. No time to investigate the church further on this particular occasion but there may be other opportunities in the weeks to come. At least I hope that there will.

Fish and Chips, Hope & Anchor.

The 'Hope & Anchor' pub in Outer Hope is well named and sits adjacent to yet another private car park that I decided to honour with my payment. Although wonderfully sunny it was still rather cool and so I decided to explore inside. At first it seemed that the place was in total darkness, such was the contrast between the light inside and out, but slowly my eyes adjusted to the gloom and there was the sought after bar and lunch menu. I was surprised how empty it was inside because I had anticipated that many visitors to the area would be on an extended Easter break but clearly it was still too early in the season for most. I selected a pint of Tribute and the predictable fish and chips. The lunch menu described the fish as 'small' and at a cost of ten pounds that was to be expected in this day and age at the most favoured tourist destinations. So I was very pleasantly surprised when my lunch arrived because in no way could the fish be described as 'small'. It seemed of a perfectly standard size to me with a good helping of chips and peas.

It is always interesting when we sit there in trepidation as we wait for our longed-for meals to arrive. Will it be yet another disappointment where what is 'described on the packet' has little relationship to what is placed in front of you. 'Is everything OK, Sir or Madam? Can I get you some sauces or condiments?' We meekly say that everything is absolutely fine when what we really mean to say is 'No, it most certainly is not OK. We definitely will not be returning!' But we don't say that and the only true reaction is that indeed we never do return to the place again. But no problem on this occasion because the fish and chips were excellent and I for one would not be complaining.

Inner Hope harbour

After lunch I wandered the short distance down to the harbour. It was low tide and somehow not as photogenic, at least to my eye, as it would have been at high tide. The sea wall had no necessity to totally enclose the harbour itself and therefore there was not that dramatic feeling associated with so many other seafaring villages in Devon and Cornwall. There every arrival and departure of a fishing boat is a perilous adventure in itself as it navigates the narrow harbour entrance. We did not stay long in Inner Hope because after the misadventures on our outward journey to the coast we still had to make the long journey back to Modbury again.

Nevertheless instead of following the direct route home we decided to take the opportunity to explore Thurlestone Sands where a palatial home had recently been constructed. Its great size seemed to be out of all proportion with the general surroundings and there was something disappointing about Thurlestone Sands but it was difficult to pinpoint exactly what it was. And then onwards we went in the South Huish direction, happily sailing along without a care in the world, until yet another beautiful old church brought us to a rapid halt.

St Andrew, South Huish.

The church of 'St Andrew' in South Huish is most certainly a ruin but what is left has been conserved by the 'Friends of the Friendless Churches'. How poetic that sounds, 'Friends of the Friendless Churches'. In my extensive random travels around the country I have come across many churches preserved by this particular charity. The church reminded me of 'St Peter the Poor Fisherman' at Revelstoke that we had previously visited in March, shortly after our arrival in Devon. However 'St Peter the Poor Fisherman' is cared for by 'The Churches Conservation Trust' but whichever charity it happens to be their work must be admired because both preserve such wonderful examples of our historic past.

And then it was once more onwards but if the truth be told I have very little understanding of where we actually went between South Huish and Churchstow. What I do know for certain is that we got lost many times in a maze of lanes and regularly we arrived at junctions where there were no signposts at all, or if there were signposts no familiar names on them. Left, right, straight over? Which way now? And then by chance a signpost for Churchstow appeared and we knew that once we arrived in the village everything would be just fine.

The lane took us into the heart of Churchstow and the map indicated that all we had to do was turn right on reaching the main road. But at the junction there was a clear 'No Right Turn' sign and so left we went down the road in totally the wrong direction until finally we could safely turn around. I had originally planned to take the shorter route from Churchstow back towards Culverwell and then on to Loddiswell. However after our previous experience of tiger traps we decided that we would not take that risk. Instead we blasted along the main highway at a heady thirty miles per hour until we finally arrived at the Leigh Cross roundabout. Then it was back on a familiar road towards Loddiswell.

It had indeed been a long a day in the saddle, at least as long as Clint Eastwood ever had to ride in his spaghetti westerns. But finally we were both back home again after having had the very good fortune to visit a number of memorable locations on a perfect sunny day. Some intended but most not. In the past I have prided myself on my map reading skills but will I ever come to terms with the devious lanes of South Devon? I simply do not think that I will. Onwards and upwards.

Chapter 13
Short, Back and Sides

It was eight o'clock in the morning. Wally Barnes had just opened up his barber shop on Tennyson Street and was busy arranging the tools of his trade for the days work. It was yet another wet, winters day outside and the streets were deserted, apart from the occasional scurrying of store staff who were already late for work. Wally had been at the shop for over forty years, initially as an apprentice, then as hired staff and finally as proud owner. He was very familiar with the fluctuations in business and he knew that today would be quiet. Too quiet for a man who had yet to fully pay off his mortgage and the college fees of his children before he retired.

At five past eight precisely a man walked into his shop. He was smartly dressed in a grey leather jacket, collar upturned against the rain, precisely pleated trousers and polished black shoes. Wally immediately noted that his hair was short and started to make his way to the counter where he sold cigarettes, nicotine patches and essentials for the weekend.

G'day. How can I help?' said Wally.

'I'd like a haircut please', the man replied. 'A number two.'

Wally looked initially puzzled but then responded,

'That'll be fine because I don't have a reservation until eight thirty. Mr Fabio is very punctual and he doesn't like to wait. If you had been one of my rock star clients with long hair I would have just had to ask you to come back later.'

It was Wally's form of a joke but the man's expression remained unchanged. Wally led the man to one of the two work positions. The other had been unoccupied for nearly two years now since he had had to let Josh go because of a lack of trade. Too much competition in a small town and his traditional business had lost out to the unisex and up market versions of his profession.

'What part of England do you come from?' asked Wally as he placed paper tissues around the collar of the man's shirt. Wally considered that he was a bit of an expert when it came to accents based on his many years experience of new migrants and tourists. He had already placed the man's origins in Newcastle, possibly Gateshead.

'Brighton', the man replied, in a dry factual response.

Wally then proceeded to expertly flourish his barber's apron like a bullfighter until it floated down precisely into position over the man's seated form.

'Have you ever been to see Brighton and Hove Albion since they moved to the Withdean?', Wally continued, trying to find a subject of mutual interest.

'Can't say that I have', replied the man and it seemed that that particular line of conversation had come to its natural conclusion. Wally had a whole stock of questions on hand but before he had a chance to commence on his second choice of subject the man spoke.

'So you're a Brechin City supporter then?'

It was hardly an inspired insight since pasted either side of the mirror were photos and posters of the Brechin City team over the years, news clippings and even Wally's supporters club membership card. Wally was thrilled since it had long ceased to be a subject of interest to his regulars, apart from the usual 'See you lost again Wal.'

'Yeah, we're in Division Two now. Still I guess we'll be relegated again this season. Usually happens. Up and down like a.....' and Wally hesitated since he had not had time to assess the man's appreciation of his bawdy humour. 'Up and down like Tower Bridge,' he continued.

'So you've been to watch them play then?' the man continued.

'No', Wally replied, 'but I plan to when I retire in a couple of years. Got a mention in the supporters club magazine two years ago. Well me and two other Kiwi jokers. Just three of us in the country.'

'So why did you choose to support Brechin City? It's a pretty unusual choice.'

'Don't know really. You've got to support someone and I guess I felt sorry for them languishing at the bottom of Scottish Division Three for most of the time. I looked them up on the map and just decided that they were the team for me.'

'So did your family originally come from Scotland then?'

'No. London. At least that's where I think they came from. Too many generations ago to be sure. No, I couldn't support your Spurs or Gunners could I. I mean where's the romance. All overpaid prima donnas as far as I'm concerned supported by overpaid city types. No give me the pie and chips brigade any day.'

Wally had by now finished with the clippers and was just tidying up the neck with his cutthroat razor. It had hardly been worth the bother since he had removed so little of the man's hair, it being already so short. Still business was business. I'll just charge him fifteen Wally decided.

It was now eight twenty eight precisely and without having to look Wally knew that in exactly one minutes time Mr Fabio would walk through the door for his usual monthly appointment. Very punctual was Mr Fabio.

Wally reached for the hand mirror and proceeded to show the seated man the fruits of his labour. The precise square neck, the perfectly clean lines.

'Can you just use a number one on the top,' requested the man, 'otherwise it tends to stand up a bit.'

Wally had not expected this since he had already drawn out the cutting process in order to give the man the impression that he was getting good value for money. Which indeed he was compared to other establishments. At that very moment Mr Fabio walked through the door. Mr Fabio was a very precise dresser, all Milan and that. God knows where he bought his clothes. Certainly not in Napier. Wally was now becoming somewhat agitated since he knew that Mr Fabio was very insistent that his haircut begin at eight thirty precisely. Mr Fabio was a very valued customer, always tipped well, but there was something about him that Wally sensed should not be trifled with. Foreign connections or something a bit unusual.

'Good morning Mr Fabio, Sir. I'll be with you immediately. I just have to finish off this gentleman. Won't be a second.'

Mr Fabio did not reply but the man in the chair could see from the reflection in the mirror that Mr Fabio was not amused. Mr Fabio had by now taken a seat from where he seemed to be staring at the back of the seated man's head with what could only be interpreted as pure disdain. How could this man ruin his day before it had barely started by taking his reserved chair.

Wally fumbled with the clippers as he tried to change the cutter heads. Finally all went smoothly and within one, perhaps two minutes at the outside, the job was finally done.

'There you are Sir,' Wally said whipping off the apron without asking for the man's approval, 'that'll be fifteen bucks thanks.'

It appeared that the man was well content with his haircut since he immediately rose from the seat and proceeded to give Wally the required payment. In return Wally handed back some more tissues for the man to remove any remaining loose hairs from his neck and then moved towards his ancient till. Without delay Mr Fabio had occupied the vacated barber's chair but the expression on his face still showed that his displeasure had not subsided. It was eight thirty two. He would make the point to Wally.

The Geordie accented Brightonian casually stood behind Mr Fabio's seated form and wiped the last hairs away from his collar. In a similar easy manner he reached inside his leather jacket and withdrew a steel grey pistol with attached silencer. For a moment Mr Fabio and the man's gaze met in the mirror and it was clear from Mr Fabio's widening pupils that the moment of recognition had arrived.

Wally had his back to the proceedings and closed the till draw with a healthy clunk. He turned and started to say

'Well nice to.....' but immediately fell silent. At that instant the bullet passed through the back of Mr Fabio's head. The man started to leave but stopped briefly to look into the remaining unbroken mirror. He casually inspected one side of his haircut and then the other. He reached into his pocket and placed an additional five dollars tip onto the counter.

'Nice job. Very nice job,' he said before casually strolling outside into the rain.

Trevor Cree
2012

Chapter 14
Footpath to California Cross

Thursday, 19th May 2022

My home in the country for this summer is located two miles from the small town of Modbury in the west and about one mile from the hamlet of California Cross in the east. No bus service passes my door and so my faithful servant, Rucio, is essential for routine shopping and for exploring the South Devon area in general.

California Cross is located on a road giving good access to Bigbury Bay, Kingsbridge, Salcombe and Slapton Sands and that seems to be the only reason why such a rural location has a petrol station and a pub, the California Inn. The petrol station has a very convenient and well-stocked Spar shop attached to it and so I usually go there every few days on Rucio to restock. The road from the campsite to California Cross is usually very quiet and initially, when the footpaths were still likely to be particularly muddy, I walked there and back along the road for much needed exercise. However directly outside of my home in the country there is a footpath that passes through the quiet little hamlet of Brownston that is to be found in a valley far below.

Initially it appears that you are walking through overhanging oak trees up a private drive to a house named Lapthorne but it is also a public right of way. After the initial driveway the footpath then descends steeply down a narrow hedge lined path towards Brownston itself. It is clear that the path acts as a channel for runoff during the winter and it is therefore eroded into small gullies with exposed stones and rocks. Finally you arrive in what seems to be the back garden of yet another house in the country and that is indeed where the footpath actually takes you, a large back garden.

Driveway towards Lapthorne.

A brilliant red rhododendron bush greeted me earlier in the year at that particular location but the flowering season has now long passed. The photographs that I have taken over a number of weeks cover the changes that have happened since I first arrived here in March, just over two months ago. Having disposed of my books on British Birds, and British Flora and Fauna, I have no way of knowing what birds, flowers, shrubs or trees I see on the way. The primroses and bluebells are always wonderful but what most of the other wild flowers are I have no idea. No doubt there is a phone App that you can simply take a photograph of a flower or record bird song and it will tell you immediately what they are but I have yet to investigate that further.

Brownston itself is situated on a lane, Chapel Down Lane, that in the westerly direction becomes so narrow that it must dissuade even local residents from using it and that perhaps explains why the hamlet has such a peaceful air. It is as if one has been transported back to the time of Thomas Hardy's novels when walking, horse, carriage and cart were the only modes of travel. There is a sense of a much slower and relaxing pace of life that invites you to pass the time of day with strangers, if there were any to be found.

Rhododendrons.

It is quite probable that half of the hamlet is now occupied by homeowners who were originally from outside of the area and who were perhaps attracted by the same peaceful atmosphere that attracts me. There appear to be at least two working farms in Brownston but the old parish church has now been converted into a private residence, like so many other churches that I have come across on my random travels throughout the country. The same fate has happened in Brownston to the Wesleyan chapel, the school and the forge.

Footpath to Brownston.

Throughout the country we see residential homes in villages and towns with the names 'The Old School', 'The Old Dairy' and 'The Old Post Office'. I guess that it is not such a bad outcome because life has changed so much and at least the buildings are renovated and the community survives, albeit it in a different form. I later read that Brownston used to be named Brownston Cross and that the lane that I am now walking used to be the main route to Plymouth from the South Hams area during the California gold rush days. It therefore must have many stories to tell.

Brownston.

After passing through Brownston the lane then rises steeply until it finally joins the main road at California Cross itself. The walk takes about thirty minutes and so it has become a very enjoyable excuse for me to have a pint of beer at the California Inn, do some shopping at the petrol station and then retrace my steps home.

The California Inn is 'open all hours' whilst the current landlord is an ex-RAF pilot of fighter jets who unusually retrained to fly Chinook helicopters at some later stage in his career. It has a very friendly atmosphere, the beer is good whilst there is a restaurant for those who wish to eat. Directly opposite the California Inn is a covered stand with an honesty box that sells home grown vegetables, eggs, bread, and pot plants. All in all, on a fine day, it is a very enjoyable walk that is forever changing. The sun is shining, it is approaching midday and so what more excuse do I need but to once again set off on foot to do some 'shopping'.

Chapter 15
Collectables

The straggling line of the Napier Art Deco Tour meandered its way past the doorway of Rosie O'Grady's. The sound of various North American accents rose and fell in harmony with their footsteps as the tour ship visitors made their way along the street towards yet another building of particular historical interest. It was a fine morning and rays of piercing sunlight tried valiantly but unsuccessfully to make an entrance into the darkest recesses of the bar. At the last moment a single figure skilfully detached itself from the rear of the file and stepped through the doorway in one flowing movement. The absence went unnoticed. For a few moments the man, for that indeed was the person's gender, hesitated, daring not to proceed further until his eyes became fully accustomed to the impenetrable gloom within.

Siobhan Keane continued drying a seemingly endless line of glasses as she closely observed the newcomer whose form was clearly silhouetted against the light. The clear signs of an expanding midriff, of an age rather closer to sixty than fifty, dressed in a lime green short sleeved shirt made of fine silk, yellow Bermuda shorts with a wide leather belt, long pink woollen golf socks and walking sandals. He certainly had no need to carry a passport.

Slowly the internal content of the room revealed itself to the man. The pool table, the darts board, the rows of wooden tables and chairs and most critically of all the location of the bar. Apart from the barmaid it quickly became apparent to him that he was the only other person in the pub, it being so early in the day.

'I take it that you are open?' he ventured as he finally made his way hesitantly towards the bar. 'I could certainly kill a Kilkenny.'

'Your timing is perfect,' Siobhan responded. 'A Kilkenny it is then.'

He could now see that she was a fine looking women, no doubt from the old country, as indeed were his own ancestors. Her complexion was dark, some remnant of the Spanish or gypsy in her genes he thought. Her hair was shiny black and fell over her shoulders, her figure full, shapely and warm.

He took a seat on a barstool and she brought the brimming Kilkenny to him.

'That'll be four dollars, thanks.'

'Frank McCarthy', he said extending his hand to her, 'from Tampa, Florida, originally from Detroit, Michigan.'

'Siobhan Keane, originally from Waterford, Ireland.'

'Pleasure to meet you Sriivvorn. So I guessed right then. You can always tell an Irish lass. And how long have you lived in New Zealand?'

Normally she was reluctant to get too involved in talking about her personal history, even with her regular customers where there was certainly no shortage of interest. But it was early in the day, so why not. She gave him his change and walked back to the sink and continued drying the glasses.

'Must be fifteen years now. I came out after college for a six month trip, drifted into Napier, met a man, and never left. Seems only like yesterday. You're off the Victoria, right?'

'Sure am. I was down that gangway before you could say Jolly Roger, or whatever you Brits say.'

'I'm not British, I'm Irish,' she responded, somewhat bridled by his lack of history.

'Sorry. No offence. My ancestors were Irish too. Yep. Left after the famine.' Equilibrium was therefore partially restored and he continued to answer her question.

'Evie and I are on a world cruise. The Queen Victoria. Don't you just love that? Left Tampa, must be eight weeks ago now. God I hate it. More like a prison hulk for octogenarians. But Evie loves it.'

'Evie's your wife then?'

He thought about this for a moment and then concluded, what the hell. She was a fellow countrywomen, at least way back when.

'No, not exactly. I'm Evie's companion, or she's mine, whatever. Evie's eighty two this year. We met at a literary lunch in Orlando five years ago. I'd written a piece for the Orlando Literary Review and it was shortlisted for an award. Never won of course. They had flown me down from the frozen wastes of Detroit for the awards dinner, just to prolong the agony I think. We were on the same table and the booze was free and so I enjoyed myself. After all it was back to the north early the next day. She must have taken a shine to me since I shared her room that night and I guess that I never left. Seems very odd now that I tell someone else.'

'So you're a writer then?'

'Nah. When I was young I thought that I could write. I had this romantic vision of being the next James, Jack or Ernest. You know, down and out on the streets of no place nowhere, writing in my freezing garret above the undertakers. Precise literary gems of genius, beauties at my feet, fame at my door, fortune just around the corner. When I was twenty two I even flew to Dublin, rented a small room, and waited. Waited for the words to flow. But there was nothing there. Well, there was plenty there but it was all just drivel. And I knew it. Hits you hard at that age, failure. Within four months I was back in Detroit working on a nothing newspaper selling ads, and occasionally, if I was lucky, writing a few paragraphs about the dog fouling issues on the south side. Writer? No lady, not me.'

'But you must have kept writing otherwise you wouldn't have met Evie in Orlando?'

'Yeh. I kept writing a bit. Twenty years of writing a bit. Submitting short stories here and there. Mostly rejected unread. But occasionally I received the odd fifty dollar cheque and the circular letter,' "Dear....enter as appropriate..... we just loved your piece on.....enter as appropriate.....Yours sincerely.....enter as appropriate. Assistant Editor....enter as appropriate." 'It's like an addiction. Somehow I can't give it up.'

The man was now momentarily lost in his thoughts, as if he were trying to answer his own question.

'So where's Evie?'

'Evie? Oh Evie never leaves the ship. This is our third world cruise and she has never left any of the ships. No ma'am. Too dangerous she says. All those rapists, murderers and terrorists around every corner. Why should she risk that? Embarks in the U S of A, disembarks in the U S of A. She's happy. As a regular client they treat her real good. Top table and all that. But me, well I'm just a collectable.'

'Sorry, I don't understand,' Siobhan asked as she reached for another glass. 'A collectable?'

'Yeh, that's right. It's what the crew call us. There must be fifteen or twenty of us on each cruise. You know, companions for much older women. They never say it to our faces of course but we know. We just feel it. Collectables that are traded in when a younger, smarter model becomes available. But what the heck, beats Detroit any day. And Evie's sweet. Widow of some guy who made it big in steel, or nuts and bolts, or something. She looks after me just fine, and we have a lot of fun. Sometimes. But what about you? You've heard my life story, for what it's worth.'

'I've told you all there is to know really. A barmaid who washes up and dries glasses. A pretty boring life. Except.' She looked at him thoughtfully. He had opened up to her, made himself vulnerable, to a complete stranger. 'Except, once I wanted to be an artist.' She paused for a moment and then continued. 'You see I studied art at college and that's all I wanted to do. Paint. Not to become famous. Not even to make a living, but just to paint. And when I reached Napier I knew that I had arrived at my final destination. It was the light that did it for me. It was the sea, the Bluff, the shade under lemon, orange and pohutukawa trees, the white painted villas peeking through deep green vegetation, the sound of music from open windows on hot summer days, the comings and goings at the port, the snow line on the Ruahines on a clear cold winters day, the pounding surf on Marine Parade, the laughter of children........' And then she stopped in mid-flow. He was watching her entranced.

He had heard her poetry, and now she had stopped. Embarrassed, she finally continued in a more formal tone.

'Then I met a guy. He was so full of life, always on the edge, exciting, spoke of revolution, the new order, we tried different drugs, absorbed the music, drank the cheap beer, made love endlessly, and had a child. It was not in his master plan you see. Fatherhood was not in his plan for the new world order. You can't join Che in the Bolivian jungle with a child, can you? You can't defeat the capitalist pigs in Berlin. And so he left. Left us alone after six months. I later heard that he ended up in Auckland. Financial consultant or something.'

'I'm sorry. I'm really sorry.'

'Don't be sorry. He was a jerk, and at the time I was as bad. It's all about being a certain age, isn't it? Now I have the best daughter in the world. She's neat and I absolutely love her to bits. I wouldn't change anything. She's at Napier Girls High, and really doing well. She's going to be a star, that one. An absolute star.'

His eyes had become fully accustomed to the dim light. It was only now, only now, that he noticed the paintings on the wall, far to his left, far to his right and the one behind him. He walked towards the first painting. It was approximately one metre square, as they all were, large and imposing. It was of fallen autumn leaves, a myriad mix of colour, impressionistic yet real, with the appearance of oils but actually watercolour. No light shone on the paint but he could feel it's richness and depth. He therefore asked her to turn on the lights that were located above each painting. The mounting matched the painting perfectly, as did the frame. He moved on to the next one, of daisies, the next of lilies, the next of sunflowers, and so on, all equally impressive, all equally distinct, all beautifully rendered.

'They're yours, aren't they. They're yours and they are absolutely beautiful. Stunningly beautiful. You are a talent, that's to be sure.'

She did not answer him but he knew.

'But why here, in Rosie O'Grady's? So gloomy and dark. They can never be shown at their best.'

'The customers prefer the low lighting and I can understand that. The boss let's me hang them for free and so I can't complain. And he only wants fifteen percent.'

'Have you sold many?'

'Nope. The people I serve are not at all interested in art. Football, golf, women but art? No. And why should they. They're a great crowd and we have a lot of fun.'

'But five hundred dollars each. That's a steal. Five hundred NZ, right, not US?'

'That's right.'

'Well Sriivvorn, there's just no justice in this world. But whatever you do keep painting, you hear. You just keep painting. Promise?'

'If you keep writing, I promise.'

'It's a deal.'

At that very moment the Art Deco Tour was passing the door in the reverse direction and with that the man said a hasty farewell, slipped out of the door and on to the end of the line, his absence unnoticed.

'Promise,' he shouted through the door one more time.

'I promise,' she replied into thin air.

The following week Siobhan took time off with her daughter but on the subsequent Monday she arrived for work at precisely eleven o'clock as usual. Even her own eyes took time to adjust to the gloom as she made her way by instinct to the bar. One hour of cleaning up and washing glasses before opening at twelve. On the counter was a note from Brad, her boss, informing her that her pay cheque for the previous month was in the till. She reached in and withdrew the envelope but as she did so she noticed another envelope addressed to 'Sriivvorn Keane, c/o Rosie O'Grady's, Hastings Street, Napier.' The stamp had a Christchurch postmark. She opened the envelope and read:

'Dear Sriivvorn, It was great meeting you the other day. Sorry about my rapid departure but the Queen Vic departed for Wellington that afternoon and I had to catch the boat you understand. Enclosed is a cheque for US$ 12,000. When the paintings arrived Evie said that it was a big steal and I had no right to pay so little for the six paintings. She said that she was angry with me but I know that she was very very pleased since Evie always gets a lot of satisfaction from a real good bargain. After all Evie is

always looking for collectables. Now keep painting, you hear, Sincere regards, Frank.

P.S. Funny thing is I started a short story this morning. And you know what, it's not bad. Not bad at all.'

Siobhan looked up from the letter. And where once there were six paintings on the walls now there were just their faded outline. And tears fell on to the letter, and the ink ran, the written words smudged and lost their meaning. They were tears of joy, they were tears of gratitude, they were tears of a new beginning.

Trevor Cree
2012

Chapter 16
Footpath To Modbury - May

Sunday, 22nd May 2022

It was a fine sunny day and so I decided to follow the footpath to the small town of Modbury which is situated approximately two miles distant from my 'mobile' home in the country. It was only the second time that I had undertaken that particular walk which takes one hour in each direction through the rolling Devon countryside. It soon became apparent that changes had clearly happened during the intervening period as the crops had grown and the flowers had changed with the season. The footpath passes through two farms on the way but the route is very well marked and no one seems to mind strangers passing by.

The local stile is very special because it often just consists of a great slab of rock and I guess that the same may be used in Cornwall, or perhaps it is unique to Devon? In places the route crosses directly over fields and some farmers have kept the width of the path clear of crops whilst other paths have only been kept open by usage.

Stone Stile.

The predominant crop seems to be barley with its long distinctive ears, green at the moment but in a month or two they will be yellow/brown and ready for harvest. When crossing one particular sea of barley I had a brief encounter with a fair maiden with her spaniel who seemed dressed for a different age. Perhaps she was from a different age. Because the path was so narrow I stood aside in one of the tramlines, we had a few pleasant words, said goodbye, never expecting to see each other again. Some ninety minutes later I did meet her again on the lane out of Modbury. We stopped once more, chatted for a while and then parted. It all reminded me of the 1945 film 'Brief Encounter' that starred Trevor Howard and Celia Johnson.

Footpath through barley in early Summer.

During my time in Modbury I went to the local Co-op to do my shopping after which I decided to investigate the Exeter Inn, the only pub in the town that I had yet to visit. The Exeter Inn is reputedly 14th century and from the street it looks very limited in size. However it actually extends back a considerable distance and has a surprisingly large sunny garden where I had no choice but to sample a pint of their own Exeter ale.

It was midday on a Sunday but like everywhere in the vicinity it was surprisingly quiet and I guess that the whole population of the UK has gone to Spain. I started chatting to the only other people in the garden and they were a couple who had recently moved down from Berkshire to live in Modbury. They seemed to absolutely love the town and it appears that a lot of their friends from Berkshire do as well and so they are never short of company. Modbury does indeed seem to have a very welcoming feel to it and a strong sense of community.

I have recently been reading that Elon Musk has made a massive multi-billion dollar bid to take over Twitter and on my walk I believe that I came across what might be examples of his first investments. One of the red boxes is located on the junction with Donkey Lane, just outside of Modbury, whilst the other is further along the same road in an easterly direction. I assume that they just appeared overnight. It seems to be a method of sending messages to friends and relations anywhere in the world and requires no investment in computers, printers or broadband facilities. From what I understand you write your message with plant based ink, using a feather quill, on a plant based product called paper.

Postbox and Donkey Lane.

The system is fully encrypted by using what they call an envelope within which you place your message and then seal the envelope so that there is no way that anyone else can see what you have written during transit. It can be double-encrypted by signing across the sealed flap of the envelope thereby making it tamper proof. There is a payment of course and that is made by buying a stamp of the required value at your nearest Elon Musk post office to stick on to the envelope. It is early days but somehow I believe that this new technology might well catch on. I have used the system once and my stress levels were much reduced. It may mean that we are no longer inundated every minute of the day by advertisements, emails and messages selling us stuff that we feel obliged to delete immediately.

Modbury.

Modbury is situated in a valley that is surrounded by hills. Therefore in order to retrace my steps I had to climb a very steep hill out of the town. I would not say that you would have to rope up to make the climb but I would imagine that in winter it would be sensible to wear a pair of crampons. Or at least if you have had a pint or two of beer. However on reaching the top of the hill without stopping it was then fairly easy going all the way home. I was rather proud of my solo ascent even if it wasn't in winter.

Chapter 17
Millennium Sunrise

It was the last minute of the last hour of the last day of the last year of the second millennium. Two young people lay on the sloping black sand beach directly adjacent to the Edgewater Motel wrapped in a single unzipped sleeping bag. It had been a cool summers evening but fortunately Napier had been spared the rain and clouds that had afflicted much of the country, thereby ruining months of preparation for the big moment.

Earlier in the evening the pair had watched the sun set blood red over the distant Ruahine Range. It had seemed as if the end of the world was at hand. The main millennium celebrations were being held at the sound shell directly opposite the Masonic Hotel. The two had mingled with the vast crowds and listened to the sounds of bands and the excited chatter of expectation. Young children skipped through the legs of parents and strangers alike. It was an unforgettable occasion but nevertheless, shortly before ten, the couple had left the main gathering and walked a kilometre or so along the beach to the spot which they had previously selected for their personal and hoped-for private moment. They could still vaguely hear the music rising and falling on the light breeze but it was now largely masked by the rhythmic sound of a light swell caressing the beach. Chomp...Swooosh. Chomp…..Swooosh.

The couples relationship had not always been so intimate. They met some five months before in a Te Anau backpacker. It was 2.00 a.m. in the morning and Ibrahim, the young man in question, had been fast asleep in a dorm with bunk space for eleven others. Suddenly the door had been flung open and uninvited light and noise invaded the space, where seconds before all had been quiet.

'Wow, great night, great night,' the man who was first to enter the room had boomed without any consideration for the other backpackers that lay within. To compound the situation the same person had switched on the main room light revealing five reclining forms within, one of whom was Ibrahim.

'Party poopers,' he continued as six of his companions also entered the room with a similar disregard for the existing occupants.

Ibrahim lay there, his face now turned away from the light, hoping that soon the noise and mayhem would subside. By now one or two of the others in the room had awoken. In the far corner were two Swedish girls, above Ibrahim was a British man, but the nationalities of the remaining two occupants were unknown to him, possibly German or Dutch.

Ibrahim was fully aware that you had to give and take when staying in backpackers. After all you weren't paying Hilton prices. You had to expect the occasional roommate who had drunk too much and the inveterate snorer who would ruin the nights sleep for everyone but him or herself. Usually it worked out just fine. But not this time. It was as if this particular group had no sensitivity of the needs of others, as if they, and only they, were of substance, of note. For them it was their earth that revolved around the sun.

By now all of the original occupants were awake. Occasionally one would turn over and exclaim a loud *hrrumph* in the hope that the message would be understood but it had no impact The late arrivals continued to talk loudly and by now they were swigging bottles of beer and munching on half cold french fries. Finally Ibrahim had had enough. He quietly unzipped his sleeping bag, swivelled his legs around, and stood up in his undershorts and teeshirt.

'Hey guys. Do you mind calling it a night. There are others in this room who are trying to sleep.'

At first the group could not quite comprehend that someone had spoken to them. And when they saw the slight young man standing before them, of obviously Middle Eastern origin, they were even more astonished. Three of the young men stood up, and the obvious leader, retorted, 'Bloody raghead. What the hell is your problem?'

'I just requested that you think of others, turn out the lights and go to bed. As simple as that.'

'Requested. Requested. Bloody Turk requests that we go to bed. Are you a tosser or what?' Ibrahim just stood there. He would not yield an inch. He would not return to his bunk until the matter was resolved one way or the other. By now the two remaining men in the group had also stood up, obviously taking a liking to the odds. Ibrahim could have gone to the backpacker reception but he knew it would be unmanned by now but he could have woken up the duty receptionist. But he would not. He would resolve it here. He would resolve it now.

The ringleader of the group advanced, having clearly decided that an important lesson had to be taught. Ibrahim stood his ground even though none of the original occupants of the room had come to his aid. Some even turned over and pretended that the situation did not exist.

'Stop it! Stop it! This is ridiculous.' It was a girl that Ibrahim had not noticed before. She was slight in stature, olive skinned in complexion but clearly steely in determination. She was, it was true, one of the group, but in the preceding period she had kept herself to herself and had already made her way to her bed.

'Yoshi! He's right. We've no right to make such a noise. It's been a great night. Now let's all calm down and go to bed.'

'This raghead insulted me Rachel. No raghead insults me. He has to pay. Like all the others.'

'He did nothing of the sort. He simply asked you to go to bed. Now grow up Yoshi. Grow up or go back home.'

She then turned to Ibrahim. 'I apologise for my friends. We've all just arrived in New Zealand and we've had a particularly hard time at home lately. It's been pretty bloody. Please forgive us. We meant no harm.'

Ibrahim looked at her without feeling. She was the enemy. She had always been the enemy. Whichever way you dressed it up. He looked each of them in the eye individually, unblinking, for some time. There was no more to be said. He turned and returned to his bunk. The group did likewise in silence. A short while later the light was turned off and an uneasy calm settled over the room. A lull in hostilities.

The next morning Ibrahim rose at six and quietly removed his rucksack to the kitchen area. He had planned to move on early the next day since his aim was to walk the Kepler Track, if hut spaces were available. He would only find out once he had visited the Department of Conservation office.

A few minutes later the girl from the night before entered the room lugging a rucksack that seemed far too large for someone so slight. She was somewhat bedraggled and it was clear that she was still half asleep. She had not noticed him and seemed to be on remote control, moving from shelf to shelf, gathering a cup here, a spoon there, and a plate from below. Their paths met at the gas cooker where Ibrahim was preparing some boiled eggs for breakfast. They did not speak. Ultimately they sat on separate tables some distance apart.

It was some time later, just as she was finishing her yoghurt, that she heard the word, 'Thanks.' At first she thought she was still dreaming since she had always been a late riser and this ungodly hour was the absolute pits. It was then that she realised that the word emanated from the young man opposite. She looked up. There was no smile on his face. No lightening of mood. But the olive branch had been extended and she took it.

'You're very welcome. It was a stupid situation. Men!'

They spoke no more.

Some time later Ibrahim made his way along the shores of Lake Te Anau and he had been particularly fortunate in being able to book his place on the Kepler. He checked his food supplies and then headed out to the start of the track. He had never walked a track before but it did not hold any fears for him. There could be few leaner and fitter than he. And hardship had been his life story.

He had been in New Zealand for barely three weeks and the contrast with his homeland could not have been more stark. Barren scrubland interspersed with the occasional orchard, olive grove or sparse wheat field had given way to a country of lush greenery, wide flowing rivers and snowy mountains. He had not known what to expect on his arrival, just the fact that he had to travel as far as he could from his homeland in search of redemption. In search of understanding. In search of, in search of what he did not quite know. The tensions that he had known for a lifetime had day by day eased but he knew that it would be a long and tortuous process, with no guarantee of success. He was searching for Ibrahim, the son of Abraham.

For the first few kilometres the track followed the shores of Lake Te Anau, shaded by mountain beech. And then it abruptly turned left and upwards, ever upwards, until he could feel the sweat on his back and the ache in his limbs. He had never felt better, not even on those secret training camps in Yemen, when he was serving the cause. At last he broke through the tree line which yielded views to the mountains beyond. And he was alone and free. For a moment in time he was his own true self, the naked child brought screaming into the world barely twenty years before. He lay back on the tussock grass whilst a hawk glided by on the midday thermals, looking for prey.

He arrived at the Luxmore Hut at three in the afternoon. He had barely made himself a cup of tea when in through the main door came the young women of the morning and the night before. It seemed that, however hard he tried he could not shake off his past. She was clearly as surprised as he and he had the impression that, if she had had the energy, she would have walked straight on to the next hut some six hours distant. But she could not and did not.

'Whether we like it or not it looks as if we're landed with each other again. At least for one night. My name is Rachel.'

He looked at her warily, and finally responded, 'Hi, my name's Ibrahim. The others…..'

'Don't worry. I'd had my fill of them all, loud sods. The only reason we were together in the first place was because we served in the same reservist unit and were demobbed at the same time. Ten days here with them was more than enough and last night I finally decided to strike out on my own.' She felt that she had already said more than she intended but it would take an idiot not to have realised her origin.

'So do they pay for you to come to New Zealand after you have done your time? I had not realised that.'

'Here and a few other countries. I guess they feel that we deserve it. And you're originally from…?'

Ibrahim looked at her closely. He could have easily said Jordan, he could even have said England, so good was his English, but he did not. 'Palestine. I'm from Palestine. Hebron.'

She had known it all along. Since he had stood up confronting her colleagues without fear. With contempt in his eyes. With hatred in his heart.

'I knew that you were. Well, we can't take our war to another land. Can we?'

'No. I think that we've both had enough of that. Do you play chess?'

She replied in the affirmative and soon the pocket chess set was in place and the game began. The pieces were moved with deliberate care, with a view to danger, with a view to advantage. And so it was with their conversation. Probing, questioning, withdrawing, advancing, until by the end of the evening they seemed to know more about each other then they could have believed just a few short hours before. By now the hut was crowded with other trampers but they had hardly noticed.

'What would you say if I said, why don't we walk together tomorrow?' said Ibrahim.

'If you said that I would probably say yes. It would seem silly to make a point of avoiding each other. Just to the end of the track. Agreed?'

'Agreed.'

That night they slept in separate bunk rooms. They met, as agreed, for breakfast at 7.00 a.m.

It is difficult to explain how hatred turns to love. They could not explain it themselves. But over the following days and weeks, they grew closer together. They shared cold and rain, they supported each other in their separation from their families and loved ones, they held each other in their nightmares, they laughed together at their failings, they cried together, they hurt together, they made love together, until, out of the forge of emotions they became one. It is difficult to say precisely when this occurred but one day on the Routeburn track they sat looking down into the valley below. Rachel was looking straight ahead at the snow covered mountain peaks opposite and in a hesitant voice she said.

'I have killed one of your brothers. It was near one of the checkpoints to Gaza. About three in the morning. I had been trained in my first year as a sniper. Never thought that I would ever have to use my skills. But we detected him from a distance. The buried microphones. The night sights. The heat sensing devices. He kept coming on. He just kept crawling towards our position. I could see his face clearly through the sights. He just had to turn around and all would be well. He must. But he kept coming. My sergeant looked at me without saying a word. I could see the reflection of the moonlight in his eyes. I squeezed the trigger. And he was no more. I have killed a man.'

'I have killed your sister,' continued Ibrahim without delay. 'It was in the north. It was a weak point in the frontier. We had carefully removed the mines and cut the wire over a number of days. We travelled swiftly to our target, a simple farmstead. The husband was not at home. I remember her face. She was like my sister. But I killed a woman. I have killed a woman.'

They turned to each other, held each other, and wept. It was their final secret. There would be no others. They had found their peace. They had found absolution. They had found their truth. They had stood before their individual Gods.

In the following weeks and months they travelled throughout the country. They loved the country like no other and they had decided that this was the one place, the only place in the world that they could live and raise a family. The past was the past. The future was the future.

But as time passed they slowly realised that they were forever tainted by their history. Chance encounters with their fellow nationals resulted only in scorn. The accidental sight of another atrocity headline, by one side or the other, only hurt them more. The letters from their families initially pleaded for them to reconsider, begged them to refrain, until finally blood ties were cut for ever. It was a matter of honour.

In a few days their visas would expire. They had no homeland to return to. They could perhaps claim asylum and had no doubt that they would be successful. But they knew it was futile. They both knew that the world had rejected them. This world was not made for them. They would have to find another place, in another time, in another space. They had agreed what to do.

As the first signs of the new dawn broke they sat up from their reclined position. The light of the unseen sun coloured the lower margins of passing clouds on the far horizon with a vivid mixture of red, purple and orange.

They turned to face each other, and then, without a word they rose and walked naked hand in hand to the seashore. The gently lapping waves rose steadily up their bodies and still they walked, towards the yet unseen sun. Still moving, moving. towards their destination, their heads finally sank below the waves and they were gone. And at that moment the golden orb broke through the rim of the earth and rapidly flooded the space with beams of light. It was a new millennium. It was a new beginning. It was a new world.

Trevor Cree
2012

Chapter 18
Footpath to Modbury - July

Sunday, 24th July 2022

My current life near to Modbury remains very satisfying and I have been taking part in the regular events of the Modbury Creative Writing Group and the South Hams Authors Network. It all sounds very grand but it is simply a collection of authors who, like myself, enjoy writing and discussing what they are doing with others of a like mind.

In late June I returned to Sussex for just over two weeks for my motorhome and moped MOTs, helped a good friend move home, and caught up with the seemingly interminable legal proceedings of the equivalent of the Jarndyce v Jarndyce case. I am hoping to spend from November until March in Cornwall but we will just have to see how that develops.

Surprisingly it is just over two months since I wrote my previous travelogue but last Friday I once again took the opportunity to walk to

Modbury and back via my usual footpath through the rolling countryside. Generally I use Rucio for my regular shopping trips to town but when the weather is fine the walk is always rewarding because the landscape constantly changes from week to week.

Drystone wall.

One of the great benefits of walking on your own is that it is very relaxing and it takes you back to a bygone age when the footpaths of our country played such an essential role in daily life. The agricultural labourers and household servants living close to where I am now living would most probably have walked to Modbury at least once or twice a week carrying their produce and handicrafts for sale, visiting the local market, buying a few essentials and returning home by the same route. What is particularly noticeable is that time slows to walking pace. In an age of the car, train, bus, aeroplane, 24/7 news and computer based everything that peace is often difficult to attain. Everyone leads such hectic lives nowadays, even in retirement, and there are very few opportunities to truly relax.

Barley bales in a Devon landscape.

I know that on my return journey on foot I will have no alternative but to carry my purchases home, just like they did a few hundred years ago. No doubt the paths were much busier then and people would stop to talk with others, catch up on the local news and gossip, and then continue on with their journey enriched by the added knowledge that they could subsequently pass on to others. You might even call it the original 'information highway'.

But on Friday I saw not a single person to exchange the time of day with and that actually had its own advantages. The only photograph that I took provided clear evidence that the barley had been harvested and all that remained were large round bales patiently waiting their turn for collection. For me the photograph illustrates a typical English landscape and I can almost hear Vaughan Williams being played in the background.

Surprisingly the wheat at West Leigh Farm had not been harvested even though the grain itself was was bullet hard and ready to be brought home. Perhaps the hired combine harvester was not immediately available or perhaps the lack of rain had meant that the grain had not filled out sufficiently and possibly it would never fill out sufficiently? Only time would tell.

Footpath through mature barley.

I had previously passed this way on the 19th June and by chance I had met the owner of West Leigh Farm who had informed me that after more than 150 years in his family he had sold the farm. A very difficult decision no doubt with so many generations of history to recount, trials and tribulations, births, marriages and deaths, hard times and good times. Crop prices are very healthy at this particular moment in time and perhaps it was right for his family to sell and seek another life? But very sad for all that. Back in June the barley and wheat were still maturing. The wheat was still green but the barley was ripening nicely either side of the clearly demarcated pathway. Beef cattle, light brown and white in colour, grazed contentedly in the meadow nearby.

Daisies in Modbury.

On arrival in Modbury it was the Co-op as usual to check on my bank balance (where does it all go?) and then the purchase of essential 'survival rations', including a bottle of Marlborough sauvignon blanc (Perhaps that is where it all goes?). A bronze hare waits for its new owner in the Brownston Gallery but the expression on its face indicated that it had been waiting for quite some time.

Then, like the agricultural labourers of old, a visit to the pub was obligatory after such a long walk. The Exeter Inn was closed at lunchtime and so it was the short trek up the hill to the always welcoming Modbury Inn. The extensive garden is always a pleasant surprise with its spirit lifting yellow parasols on a bright clear blue sky day.

A pint of Tamar ale and soon duty called and it was back to the foot of Galpin Street where the mighty hill stood once more in my path. As noted previously roping up is recommended but because I was on my own there was no option but to put one foot in front of the other until Donkey Lane was passed and soon the summit was reached without the need for a single stop. I guess you could say the climb is the equivalent of my monthly health check because I was never out of breath and in fact I continued all the way home without pausing. Sounds like famous last words to me.

The Brownston Gallery, Modbury.

Chapter 19
Napier Lights

The two ship's engineers lent against the railings and observed the twinkling lights of Napier in the far distance. Their ship had anchored barely one hour before after a long voyage from the other side of the world. Hull in England to be precise, via the Panama Canal. They were both novices at the seafaring game having joined the P & O shipping company as eighth engineers barely nine weeks before. The interviews in a smart London office, the fitting of officer uniforms, provisioning of other day to day clothing requirements, the safety training down at HMS Vernon in Portsmouth and before they knew it they were both walking up the gangway to join the M.V. Tekoa, a wild reefer bound for New Zealand.

It was all a bit daunting at first since, although they had completed their engineering apprenticeships and were qualified maintenance fitters, the ship's engine room was initially a complete mystery to them both. Jim was immediately assigned the eight to four shift whilst Tom had been given the four to midnight. They had been lucky with their engine room supervisors since the fourth engineer, Ron, was a good hearted cockney type and a West Ham supporter, whilst Tom's supervisor Robby, the fifth engineer, was a broad accented Glaswegian, impossible to understand, but with a very good heart. Fortunately they had kept clear of the bastard second and third engineers, both bullying Scots from the Gorbals, who liked the bottle a little too much.

The two newcomers did not see a great deal of each other during the six week voyage because when Jim was coming off his shift Tom was just starting his. However the officers bar was still open after midnight and on occasion they would share a beer and a game of darts together before calling it a night. As the darts flew through the air they were able to share work experiences and discuss what they had learned down in the engine room below. And there was a great deal to learn. Valves and gauges, bilges and pipes, pistons and cylinders, generators and compressors, a maze of complications. At other times they talked about their families at home and the lives that they had led before they had joined the merchant marine. With the passing of days they became good friends.

Sailing out of the English Channel, watching the west country coastline sink finally below the horizon, crossing the Atlantic in good weather and bad, fuelling at Curacao with no time for shore leave, transiting the steamy Panama Canal, all Gauguin like and threatening. Sweeping past the Marquesas and Society Islands so close to the waves breaking on the coral reef, and then the first sight of the long white cloud caressing the slopes of the Ruahines. And then there was nightfall as the anchor was dropped.

Tom was on the evening shift and so he had climbed up from the engine control room and into the funnel, on the pretext of checking the boiler water level and safety valve. As he opened the funnel door fresh evening air blew in giving him some relief from the heat below. Jim also had the idea of climbing up to the same vantage point via the external access way.

'Whad'ya think,' said Tom. 'Do you know when we are we going to dock?'

'Nobody seems to know. It's a little secret that the captain and first engineer like to keep to themselves. I guess it depends on when a wharf becomes free. They say that sometimes we can stand off for days.'

'God I hope not,' said Tom, 'I'm dying to get ashore. It seems like years since we left Hull.'

'Same here. Can't wait to sink a few beers and chat up a few of the local girls.'

Tom did not reciprocate those sentiments but continued, 'So we're on twelve hour shifts in port.'

'So they say. Gives us more time to have a bit of shore leave. Still it's a long slog, twelve hours.'

It so happened that they entered port early the next morning and Jim had been given the initial noon to midnight shift. Just his luck. When all the others were partying in town he would be stuck in the engine room being bored to tears. Oh well. It would be his turn the next day. It was indeed a long slow shift down below but the clock was by now approaching ten in the evening and soon he would be free to have a shower, a quick beer and finally crash out for the night on his own double bed. It was one of the perks of being an officer, your own large room and ensuite facilities. Having a personal steward also helped. He was contemplating this scenario when he looked up and saw that Tom was unsteadily descending the engine room stairs closely followed by another form, a female form. It was clear that Tom had had more than a few beers and that the party had moved from town to the officers bar on board.

'I'd like you to meet.....I'd like you to meet....' Tom slurred. 'Sorry darling, what's your name?'

'Emily.'

'That's right. Course it is. I knew all the time. And this is Jimmy.'

Tom had never called Jim that before.

'Emily's a doctor, aren't you Emily? A doctor.'

'I'm a nurse. A nurse at the Napier General.'

Up until this point Jim had not said a word. He was in a trance. He had never in his short life seen such a beautiful girl. The heat of the engine room, the deafening roar of the generators, even Tom no longer existed. Jim was immediately besotted. That strange, magical, and oh so rare feeling. It was certainly not the wafer thin classic beauty of a magazine model that he saw before him. She might not even turn other heads. But for him she was beauty personified, and they hadn't even spoken. The sweetest of features with long tumbling locks of shoulder length fair hair, piercing blue eyes and a full figure. And a smile like no other.

'Emily wanted to see the engine room, and I know it's against the rules but I .... I..... Now where was I. That's right. That's right. I wanted her to meet my very very best mate in the whole world. I wanted her to meet Jimmy. Because I luv him, don't I Jimmy. Yeh. I luv him more that any other.'

Jim looked at Tom's unsteady form before him and laughed. 'Yeh, that's right Tom.' It was immediately clear to Jim that he had better guide them both up to the accommodation level at once before Tom got into deep deep trouble. He placed Tom's arm over his shoulder, grabbed his waste and step by step virtually carried him up four decks. Although it was against regulations he left the engine room and carried Tom's dead weight into the room adjacent to his own, just a few yards along the corridor.

'He'll be alright now,' Jim said to Emily. 'Look after him.'

What an absolute disaster Jim concluded as he returned down below. My own mate has hitched up with the most beautiful woman in the world and there's absolutely nothing I can do about it.

By the time that Jim had finished his shift and finally handed over to the other eighth engineer, Geordie John, the party onboard had moved away from ship to shore. The Cabana someone had said. The ship's bar was empty but he still had a chilled bottle of Brewmaster. After that it was straight to bed in the knowledge that Emily and Tom were most probably entwined in the bed next door.

But tomorrow would be his day. Then he could party. But for a long time he just could not get to sleep. He could not help thinking about Emily sharing Tom's bed. If there was one person on the ship that Jim could accept that to happen to it was Tom, but it certainly didn't make it any easier. It hurt like nothing he had ever experienced before. Just my luck he thought, getting the first long shift.

Just before midday Jim entered the dining room to see that Tom was just finishing his lunch prior to starting his own long afternoon and evening shift. He looked awful.

'Hey Tom. You look absolutely stuffed.'

'You don't have to shout,' said Tom quietly. 'God I feel awful. I promise that I will never ever drink another bottle of beer, or vodka, or rum, ever ever again. On my father's grave.'

'Your father's not dead Tom.'

'Well on somebody else's grave then.'

'How's Emily?' It was not a question that Jim wanted to ask but he knew that he had to have the answer.

'Fine I think. Can't remember much actually. She left this morning. Had to go to work or something.'

'You'll be seeing her again then?'

'Not sure. The truth is I can't remember whether we arranged anything. Well I've got to go now, down into depths of hell. You don't have a bucket full of aspirins do you Jim?

Jim left the ship at three in the afternoon in the company of two young apprentice navigating officers. Although they were much younger than Jim they already had a number of years experience of the various fleshpots of the world. And they could honestly say that they had been cheated in all of them. It was just how things were when you had had a few beers and had a very limited time in which to enjoy yourselves. Occasionally they ran into other members of the ship's crew, greasers, deck hands and the like, coming out of places of ill repute with one, sometimes two women of character on their arms. Jim thought that some of the women were old enough to be their mothers but it didn't seem to faze them at all.

At that point Jim's two companions said they had been invited to a party on the hill. Cameron Road. Everyones invited. Why not come along.

'Sounds great. Lead on Horatio.'

They had a rudimentary street map of Napier and at last found Tiffin Park and began the long climb up the steps through the trees. It was a pretty steep incline by any measure but before long they had reached the top and were soon entering Cameron Road.

'What number is it,' asked Jim.

'Don't know. The nurses we met last night just said follow the music.'

And that is exactly what they did. Just a few hundred metres down the road. It was a beautiful traditional villa, somewhat run down, but full of character. The garden was full of native shrubs, lemon trees, with cool shaded areas for respite from the searing January sun.

And standing at the door, standing perfectly framed by the door, stood Emily. Smiling, radiant.

'Hi, how are you. Jimmy, isn't it?'

'Jim actually. Tom was a little out of it last night. I'm not sure where Jimmy came from. Great place. Do you live here?'

'Yes I do. Myself and a few others. Beer?'

'Love one.'

Emily showed Jim around the whole house and one by one introduced him to her housemates. They were certainly an interesting bunch, all good types, most working, some not, male and female, late teens, early twenties. Santana was blasting out of the windows and over the rooftops beyond into a sultry afternoon.

It is difficult to say what happens when two lovers collide. Perhaps they are enveloped in a bubble because they are totally oblivious to what is happening beyond the gossamer thin film. And so it was with Jim and Emily. The hours passed. The party swirled around them. Pink Floyd gave way to Cat Stevens. Cat Stevens to the Stones and then to Joni. Afternoon to dusk, dusk to darkness. And then they wanted to stay together. But it was not so easy.

'Emily. I'm not sure how I can put this so that you will not be offended.'

'You mean did I sleep with Tom? Did we make love?'

'No. Well Yes. God I don't know. It's just that I'm experiencing such strong feelings. Irrational, mad feelings. We've known each other for just a few hours. It just doesn't make any sense at all. But most of all I don't want to cause you hurt. It happens too often. I'd rather we just became good friends rather than hurt each other. I need to know how you feel. Honestly.'

'It's a strange thing', Emily began. 'When I descended into the engine room it was such an alien place. Tom had had a few and insisted that I met you. And I saw you. And.......And I fell for you there and then. We never said a word. We never exchanged a single word. And then we were climbing. And Tom had been so good, protecting me from those older drunken engineers, with their innuendo and spite. So I lay with him. We never made love, he was too far gone, and anyway I would not have. I just lay with him until the morning and left. He's different, have you not noticed? Women can sense these things.'

And so it was settled. They felt exactly the same. But first Jim had to tell Tom. He could not betray a mate. He had to explain the situation face to face. To tell him that…well, how else to explain it, he had fallen in love. If Tom smacked him on the chin he would not have reacted. It was far less than he deserved. Emily did not have to join him, but she insisted. And so they walked hand in hand down the hill and along Breakwater Road to the ship.

It was just after ten when they descended into the engine room where Tom was both surprised and pleased to see them both. It was a surreal situation, Jim standing there, the deafening sound of generators, explaining from his heart what had happened, how the last thing he wanted was to hurt Tom, that he had to tell him first hand, how he could not have secretly cheated on him. And then it was over. There was no great fuss. It was as if Tom had been stunned. He just said, 'Well,.....I understand.'

And then they left, ascending the way they had come, higher and higher, and out into the sea breeze. On the way home to Cameron Road they did not speak. There was nothing to be said. They were both subdued by the enormity of what they had done. Betrayal is hard. Betrayal is cruel. And that night they made love as if it was for the very first time in their lives.

Over the following days Jim and Tom hardly spoke. In fact they rarely saw each other apart from when they handed over their shifts to each other. Technical, factual reports, their former relationship now no more. And every spare moment Jim spent at Cameron Road whilst his bed on the ship remained unoccupied, its clean linen untainted.

On the fourth day Jim lay listening to the early morning birdsong, wrapped in the warmth of his lover. In the distance the sound of a ship's klaxon sounded through the valleys of Bluff Hill. Once. Twice. And he knew that his ship would soon be leaving. And he knew that he would be staying. It was where he belonged. It was where his life was now beginning.

And in the far distance a man leant against the ship's railing, Napier slowly disappearing over the horizon. He knew that he had lost the love of his life. It would never be the same. He would never meet anyone like him again. Of that he was certain.

Trevor Cree
2012

Chapter 20
Wonwell Beach & Kingston

Monday, 8th August 2022

It was once again a beautiful day and so on the spur of the moment I decided to take Rucio for an early morning expedition to Wonwell Beach and Kingston. Wonwell Beach is located at the mouth of the River Erme and because the estuary is sheltered it has large expanses of golden sand. The village of Kingston is located close by and since I had not visited either before it seemed to be well worth making the effort.

As usual I planned my route with military precision and as usual I very soon lost my way. Somehow I ended up on the road to Bigbury Bay but arriving at the familiar St Anne's Chapel I took a right turn in the direction of Ringmore, where I had been before, and then finally on to Kingston by the 'scenic route'. The lanes of South Devon never cease to amaze me because they are virtually impossible to navigate and yet hidden away people live on a permanent basis, like the lost tribes of the Amazonian rainforest. Elsewhere in the country the very wealthy buy large estates so that they can be far away from other people but here in Devon nobody could ever find you even if they tried, including close friends. Around every leafy corner you expect to find a family who had never met another human being since the 16th century and who would be surprised to learn that the bubonic plague was long past.

The Erme estuary.

The lack of signposts in Kingston meant that an unplanned visit to the wonderfully named Scobbiscombe Farm was undertaken before it was back to the village and then finally on to Wonwell Beach, via Blackpost Cross. The lane was so narrow that I had to ask a lady walking her dog if I was still heading in the right direction, which she confirmed. Since it was still relatively early in the morning there were very few cars parked at Wonwell Beach and in any case Rucio fits into the smallest of spaces. I had brought some water and a banana in my expedition 'survival pack' and because the tide was relatively low I was able to walk on the sand past a disused lime kiln and Malthouse Point.

There was still an incoming tide and the golden sands most certainly did not disappoint. I had decided to explore the South West Coast Path for a mile or two along the rugged cliffs as far as Fernycombe Beach. Far below the water was calm and three yachts lay at anchor, clearly intent on going absolutely nowhere that day. The views along the South West

Coast Path were indeed special and I met very few walkers and so that was a bonus. Finally I arrived on the cliffs high above Fernycombe Beach and the water was so clear you could see the outline of rocks below the surface. I believe that walking all, or more realistically part, of the South West Coast Path would be very rewarding to many but it would undoubtably be a bit of a slog with the 'big dipper' contours on most of the path.

Fernycombe Beach.

Having timed my walk to perfection it was by now opening time and so as more and more people began arriving at Wonwell I was already on my way in the opposite direction to the Dolphin Inn at Kingston. A pint of Jail ale from the Dartmoor brewery, a packet of crisps, sun on my back in the garden and all was well with the world.

The oak village notice board in Kingston had been installed to celebrate the Queen's Golden Jubilee of 2002. The forthcoming village horticultural competition entry rules were clearly outlined identifying the main categories of vegetables, preserves, fruit and eggs, flowers and so on. The fruit category specifically stated that the fruit should be *'displayed with stalks attached'* whilst the Class A vegetable categories should consist of 3 onions, 3 shallots, 3 garlic, 3 leeks, 3 beetroot and so on but only 1 lettuce. I'm not quite sure what the 'Kingston Lettuce Liberation Front' will think of that example of unacceptable discrimination? I particularly liked the 'jam jar of wild flowers' in contrast to the more formal 'vases' required for other flower entries. Wonderful memories of childhood.

Dolphin Inn, Kingston.

Our churches often have such wonderful names and 'Saint James the Less' in Kingston is a prime example. It seems that 'Saint James the

Less' was one of the twelve disciples and depending on the translation of the Greek he was known as 'the Minor', 'the Little', 'the Lesser' or 'the Younger'. Having taken a great interest in family history for many years has led me to a certain degree of understanding of the origin of surnames whereby 'George the Younger' often became 'George Younger', 'Thomas of Ashurst' became 'Thomas Ashurst' and so on. A few, through no fault of their own, have probably been landed by history with unfortunate surnames such as 'John of Piddle' in Dorset, in reference to the river of that name, becoming 'John Piddle', 'Morris the Minor' becoming 'Morris Minor' but as far as I know there are no known examples of 'Trevor the Slothful'.

Saint James the Less gateway.

The doors of 'Saint James the Less' were open when so many small churches have been forced to lock out the faithful because of anti-social behaviour. The interior was somewhat spartan but the peace of the place could be felt in direct contrast to the great cathedrals where we wander in throngs.

By now it was time to return to 'my home in the country' and this time I managed to follow the beautiful narrow lanes that I meant to take on the way out. Well nearly.

Chapter 21
Freedoms and Liberties

Jed Russell lounged back in his executive leather chair and quietly monitored the three flat screens that were ranged before him. All iMacs. Two twenty four inch and a smaller eighteen inch one in between. It could easily have been the trading floor of a major city broker anywhere in the world but the absence of expletives and noise confirmed that it was not. He was the only one in the room.

Jed had come a long way in the last three years and he was still barely out of his teens. It had been a pretty scary ride. A young kid at junior school with an interest, or more accurately, an obsession with computers. A government dumping new technology on the schools by the truckload in their desire to ride the wave and not get left behind. And he had taken full advantage. It was true that some of the basics, such as english and maths, had got left behind on the way but the school liked to nurture talent, any talent, as long as they excelled. The government inspectors were always impressed by some tiny tot playing a few bars of Elgar's Cello Concerto rather than neat, but boring, rows of pupils reciting their 12 x 12 tables.

By the time he had reached senior school Jed was a favourite with the IT teachers simply because he knew more than they did, or indeed ever would, about the subject. And best of all the technicians let him take the broken machines apart and repair them so that he became as good an engineer as he was a software programmer. It was clear to the school that Jed was going to be somebody some day. Somebody like Bill Gates or Steve Jobs who had never made it through college but had made it big. Very big.

But Jed had other ideas, much to the disappointment of both school and parents. By the time that he had left school at eighteen he was already living in another world, a virtual world, yet at the same time a very real world. Broadband access gave him the key to unlock the door from his standalone bedroom computer and provided access to a totally interconnected world. A world of millions and millions of computers, both large and small, chattering to each other in different languages, opening doors for a while and then closing them tight. Jed was fascinated by locks, as much as any safe breaker or bona fide locksmith. He always wanted to see what was behind that door and the bigger the lock the greater the challenge. And there was no greater challenge than the military. It was not as if he were after their grubby secrets since his interests at that age never extended to politics, or even to right and wrong. He was happy to leave that up to others.

Jed was well aware that he could not just knock on the door and ask to be let in. He would let his 'friends' do the job for him. Well friends was rather pushing the definition of the word since they were actually computers belonging to people and organisations that he would never meet and would never know. Layer upon layer of them, each seeded with the parasitic egg that he had laid. Each handling only a few nano bits of the full packet of information that he had abstracted. He never accessed a 'friends' computer for more than a few minutes and afterwards nobody was any the wiser. Nobody had been harmed.

The information that he collected was of momentary interest to him. Progress on the US missile shield, NZ deployments in Afghanistan, British naval exercises off Yemen and so on. His interest was never the actual content but the fact that he had broken through the encryption, had entered myriad sacred and forbidden places. His interest waned after gaining entry for the objective had been achieved and then it was on to the next door. He never passed on the information that he saw to others and was always doubly careful that any record of that information was permanently erased from his computer. And nobody knew how to erase computer evidence better than he.

And then one day, about six months after he had started this adventure, things had started to go wrong. Badly wrong. He could see them searching for him. Not outside of his parents house and the bedroom that he occupied most of the time but on the screen before him. It became dangerous to stay on his new 'friends' computers for more than a few seconds and then even less than that. And as the days passed he could see that they were getting closer and where once he had one hundred layers of separation, one hundred layers of protection, now there were only five.

He could have easily shut down his computer, taken it to the bush, and smashed it up into little pieces with a hammer, before taking the separate parts to the refuse dump in nondescript black polythene bags, one by one. After a few explanations to his parents about out of date technology he would have bought a new more advanced computer, no questions asked. They were just pleased that he was content because one day he would finally grow up and get a proper job. No doubt a very well paid job.

But he could not leave it alone. This was the big game. Who were these guys? He could still evade them yet. They had no idea what country he was in never mind what town. He tried everything he knew, laying false trails, leading them into secret Chinese and Russian sites just to slow them down for a bit and cause a temporary but unpublicised diplomatic tiff. But he could not shake them off. And then it was all over.

There was no great scene. Just two well dressed men came to the door. His parents were shocked. There was no publicity. After all there had been just a bit too much of that with the people from Langley threatening extradition and multiple life sentences over some pimply kid from Invercargill who had upset them a year or two before. No, this time the people from Wellington had got there first. Just. The Yanks and Brits never did find out who had caused such mayhem, never mind any obligations to the Five Eyes agreement. The Chinese and Russians were too concerned about a loss of face to make a fuss. Wellington just said that the trail had gone cold.

They took him from his home in Napier to Wellington. No blank prison cell wall to look at for him but a temporary four star hotel room overlooking the bay. This is the deal they said. You work for us and there will be no charges. The pay would be good and the work would be interesting, at least for a computer geek like Jed. His parents had already been taken care of on the first meeting when subtle hints had been made about his viewing inappropriate material on the internet. The words 'porn' and 'deviant' had never actually been used but there was enough there for his parents to draw the wrong conclusions. And it was certainly nothing that they wanted to discuss with their neighbours over the garden fence. No charges. Jed will be working for us in Wellington, was all they said, using the skills that they knew he had in spades. They were actually relieved since Jed would be off their hands at last and actually working for a living. That was enough for them.

It took quite a few weeks before they gave Jed anything of importance since they had to make sure that he didn't go native on them. Didn't disappear off into the blue yonder covering his tracks all the way. No, Jed was fine. Give him the very latest kit, the fastest internet connection, and he wasn't going anywhere. He was in his element, and well paid for being there as well. Homeland security they said.

Ever since 9/11 government had been pressing them for a much better handle on potential terrorist threats and how they could be covertly monitored.

And it was Jed who gave them the answer. It had been nine months before when he had been inside a Chinese site that he had found it. The Chinese-English translation software automatically provided the content whilst another piece of software that he had developed selected only specified keywords and dumped the rest. He had deduced as much even before he had the conclusive proof. That was why he had never owned a mobile phone himself. Why on earth did the Chinese government allow its citizens to have access to mobile phones? Simple really. So that they could monitor them, record conversations, and pre-empt subversion. Stability was king.

And when the West came running to them for low cost mobile phone manufacture it presented them with a golden opportunity. The mobile phone companies provided them with all the specifications for the electronic parts and low cost labour did the rest. Everybody was happy, the western telecoms companies, the Chinese manufacturers and global consumers. It was a win win situation. Except that the Chinese security services had added a little more. They knew that every phone would be ruthlessly checked for non-standard electronic components by western intelligence and so everything was always totally in order. It was just China doing business, making money, being part of the international trading community.

Apart that was from the cheap multi-coloured protective casings for the phone itself, produced in their millions. The casings that made the difference between a style icon and a broken piece of unusable merchandise. And one day Jed had unlocked a door and located the written proof within. Hidden within the perimeter of every plastic moulding was a minuscule decorative thread that transmitted every text, every word, every photo, every email, every *'And she said like,'* ever uttered. But full access to the NZ telecommunications network had yet to be achieved. It was just a trojan horse, put in place, waiting for the future. But Jed's friends in Wellington had access to the national network. Total uninhibited access. State security. Never advertised, never publicly admitted.

And so Jed set up the pilot project for them. He was in his element. It took a further two months of twelve hour days but then he had it cracked. Every mobile sold in NZ with their essential protective casing was accessible. All that was required was a testing ground. Napier. His birthplace. Why not. A port with direct international access. Small enough to be monitored, far away enough to be deniable. Rogue elements, now dismissed. Won't happen again.

And so Jed lay back in his leather chair and admired the fruits of his labour. He had now been in place on the top floor of the police building on the corner of Dalton and Station Street for four months. His room was strictly off limits to all officers, and that included the Hawkes Bay Chief. The high security swipe card access saw to that. Jed's jandal footed, jean clad and long haired arrival and departure needled everyone from the desk Sergeant to the Chief. It was not that he had ever said anything objectionable to anyone. It was just his presence and the annoying fact that nobody had any idea what he was doing. Statistical analysis of local and national crime figures was the official story. But then why all the security they asked.

The beautiful part of the system that Jed had created was that he could see and hear everything. The two main screens were full of little coloured icons, each representing individual mobile phones, on a background map of the central district of Napier. Click on an individual icon and the central screen immediately showed details of the owner and any activity related to that specific phone. Even if it was switched off Jed could hear any conversation within the immediate vicinity. The owner's driving license and associated photograph, bank records, convictions, education, workplace, unemployment history, flights taken, marriage documents, mortgages and loans, close associates and so on were all there to see.

Jed knew more about the residents and visitors to central Napier than anyone on the planet. His bosses in Wellington only knew what he told them or what he copied to them but they were more than happy with the intelligence capability that he provided. Sometimes, when he was particularly bored, he would listen into the arguments of the old couple on Seapoint Road, or the love making of the gay couple down Chaucer Street, or the smalltime transactions of the marijuana dealers at the back of the Cabana. On the screen he could see thousands of little icons, follow them into Farmers and out into Hastings Street, monitor their withdrawals from the Bank of New Zealand opposite, and observe their subsequent purchase of three towels and a pair of shorts, again at Farmers. He felt like God and in a way he was God. He had access to everything about everyone, at least within the range of the transmitters.

But this was just the sideshow entertainment. Jed's system was primarily set up to react to certain predefined keywords. His section in Wellington, CI9, was solely focussed on terrorism and directly related areas such as Class A drugs, gun running and money laundering. Virtually all of the time his icons were blue, yellow or green, indicating different levels of nothingness. It was the occasional flashing orange or red icons that were of particular interest. Action triggered by multiple keywords including the obvious ones such as Peshawar, semtex, Al Qaeda, but also certain flight numbers, phone numbers, shipping container origins and so on. It had always been a series of false alarms until now but Wellington would still dispatch a couple of it's undercover operatives to investigate any hint of subversion. The lack of concrete results was not going down well in HQ. A great deal of money had been spent on the project and certain people in government, with the appropriate security clearance, were getting impatient.

However Jed the non-political being had been having a slow awakening. The technical challenge of the last couple of years had been more than enough to keep him motivated, the pay was good and the fulfilment of seeing the system that he had developed working perfectly was hard to beat. But he had to face up to it. There was something very concerning about recent developments. Whereas previously Wellington had instructed him to immediately filter out all of the dross and just feed through the national security related data, now they kept requesting more and more peripheral information. Personal stuff. About more and more individuals. Initially it was just half a dozen of the usual Napier suspects, local petty thieves, biker gang members, smalltime pot dealers, hookers but now it was over one hundred that were regularly under surveillance with their flashing icons. Where would it all end Would it ever end? In fact what the hell was going on? It just wasn't right but his official complaints fell on deaf ears. It was then that Jed picked up that weeks copy of the Listener to see how he might pass his free time in the coming days.

At precisely 3.05 p.m. on the Wednesday afternoon all hell broke loose on the screen in one precise location. The flashing icon on Hadfield Terrace was going bananas and the icon was showing the highest state of alert, crimson. By 3.20 p.m. many of the main keywords had been activated. A complete list was displayed on Jed's central screen, and now simultaneously in Wellington. Based on the available evidence there was no time for delay and Wellington immediately authorised an armed intervention. This was the big one that they had been waiting for so long. This was the one that would keep their masters happy. The only problem was that Napier had no specialist units on hand and so Wellington had to rapidly explain the situation to the Napier police chief.

'Why the bloody hell were we not kept in the loop?' exclaimed the police chief before he slammed down the phone and rapidly got his available forces together. Within seconds he was hearing the relay through his earpiece.

'We move tonight' said a thickly accented voice. 'We take out port oil tanks in one go. Security no good, hole up few days, wait further instructions. Allah Akbar!'

There was clearly no time to be lost. The police chief jumped into an unmarked car and instructed his driver to proceed quickly, but not too quickly as to attract undue attention. Three other unmarked cars discreetly approached Hadfield Terrace from different directions carrying the only six armed officers available. It would have to be enough. The heavy brigade from Wellington would arrive by plane far too late. The Chief's car swept along Hastings Street and up Shakespeare Road.

'Phone Napier Girls High and tell them to evacuate the place. Tell them to go to the Sacred Heart......I don't care what you tell them Sergeant. Tell them there's a mad flasher on the prowl but get them out of there! Jack. Jack, you take your lads up to Coote Road to block off any exit from the rear of the property. Brett you and your lads block off the steps down to Seaview Terrace and Onslow Road......Sorry Charlene. I forgot you were on the team. I'll shout the beers when this is over. What? ......Course I've bought a round before.'

The Chief and his men got out of their cars at the entrance to Onslow Road, two of them taking the Hukarere Road, and two taking the Gladstone Road access.

'Are you ready to die for the cause?' the voice in the Chief's earpiece continued. 'I am,' said a second voice. 'God is great,' said a third.

It was a hot afternoon and fortunately nobody was on the surrounding streets, slumbering as they were in the shade. It was now 3.40 p.m.

'Right lads,' the Chief spoke into his sleeve. 'I don't want any of us to get hurt, but we have to take them out now. Murray and Jim around the back. Tom and I will go straight through the front door. That Jed freak says that they are all in the kitchen and they are still talking normally.'

It was 3.44 p.m. 'Right lads, now!'

The Chief stove in the front door with a size twelve boot and rapidly made his way along the hallway to the kitchen covering all options with his revolver. The two out the back did likewise and within an instant they had all met at an open kitchen door. And then they saw him. Lying back in his armchair, snoring to his hearts content, oblivious after a jug or two down at the Cabana. Old Frankie Groves. Former Chief Inspector Frankie Groves. And on the dresser a vintage Roberts radio sat in prime position whilst the Wednesday Play came to it's natural conclusion. And on the kitchen table lay the mobile phone which Frankie's daughter, Lisa, had bought him in case he had another turn.

It was 3.46 p.m. Jed took his bare feet off the console. 'Bloody good play that. Enjoyed it the second time round as much as the first.' And then without further delay he rose, turned back on all the other listener icons in Napier that he had temporarily blocked, left the room, locking it securely behind him. 'Freedoms and Liberties. You've got to protect individual freedoms and liberties,' he said to himself as he walked out of the police headquarters to start a new life. A better life. A more meaningful life.

Frankie Groves. Frankie Groves. The tracked phone had been registered in the name of Lisa Baker, his daughter's married name. Now that was an unexpected and welcome bonus to sign off on. Chief Inspector Frankie Groves! Now that would take some explaining to the minister.

Trevor Cree
2012

Chapter 22
Prawle Point & East Portlemouth

Friday, 9th September 2022

The weather had been particularly unsettled for a week or more with heavy downpours and in the far distance there had been the occasional rumble of thunder and flashes of lightning. The wonderful summer had finally broken and autumn was clearly just around the corner. And so when I awoke one Friday morning to a clear blue sky it seemed to be a sign from above that that day was indeed the day to head off and explore a new area of South Devon.

The larger settlements of Kingsbridge and Salcombe are located on a major inlet and it was the land to the east that had until now eluded Rucio and myself. Not that Rucio was in the least bit bothered. The planned visits for the day were to be Start Point, Prawle Point and then finally on to East Portlemouth before returning home. Rucio and I had successfully navigated the minor roads to Kingsbridge and back a number of times but beyond Kingsbridge was a bit of a mystery, And so learning from my past mistakes I wrote down on a piece of paper a precise list of all the hamlets and villages that we must pass through on this particular outing, commencing with Frogmore and then on to Herring Street, South Allington, Bickerton, Hillsands, Start Point, Prawle Point and East Portlemouth. It goes without saying that we never did see South Allington, Bickerton, the beaches of Hillsands or even one of my key locations to visit, Start Point.

Lannacombe Bay.

The village of East Prawle is the location of the wonderfully named Pig's Nose Inn, a name that was derived from the nearby Pig's Nose cliffs where iron ore mining was undertaken for a short period during the mid-1800s. Approximately two miles to the south-west of the village lies Prawle Point itself jutting out into the English Channel and throughout history its cliffs would have been a hazard to shipping.

My first view of the Prawle Point was unexpected because it suddenly appeared through a gateway set into the typical high hedges and earth banks that line so many Devon lanes. The view was magnificent and far out to sea a solitary yacht battled against a stiff breeze under the watchful eye of the coastguard station. Looking south-east the sea momentarily took on a sparkling silver hue and it reminded me of the words *'set in the silver sea'* but I could not recall their origin. I now know that the words were spoken on his deathbed by John of Gaunt (1340 - 1399) in William Shakespeare's play *Richard II*, as follows:

*'This fortress built by Nature for herself
Against infection and the hand of war,
This happy breed of men, this little world,
This precious stone set in the silver sea,
Which serves it in the office of a wall,
Or as a moat defensive to a house,
Against the envy of less happier lands,
This blessed plot, this earth, this realm, this England.'*

In an age that seems to take pleasure in denigrating everything about our history I guess that is how I feel about England. For all its faults I love this land.

Tripp inscription.

Whilst looking out at the marvellous view my eye was drawn to one of the concrete gateposts on which had been inscribed during its manufacture 'G.R.H. Tripp 1974'. I found this intriguing and so on my return home I undertook some online research. The East Prawle History Society website page included a 1954 photograph of a young Geoffrey Tripp sitting on a Ferguson TE20 tractor whilst further research revealed that there is still an active Tripp's Campsite at Higher Farm, East Prawle. I posted my photograph on the local Facebook page and within a day the mystery had been solved. It was indeed the young Geoffrey Tripp that had left his mark on history on the gatepost all those years ago and he still farms at Higher Farm.

Batson Creek, Salcombe.

We arrived in East Portlemouth from the east and the centre of the village is located high above the Salcombe estuary. The name East Portlemouth is indeed quite a mouthful and would probably elicit a follow up question of 'Where?' should an East Portlemouth resident be asked where they lived. 'No Portlemouth, not Pottymouth.' A small car park invites, but does not demand, donations towards the upkeep of the village hall and I duly made my contribution even though we stayed for just a few minutes.

An adjacent hand written sign advertised electric bikes for hire at £40 per day and if I had brought my own board I would have set up shop there and then and offered to carry customers on my back for a bargain £35 per day. There was clearly no point my offering the services of Rucio who would have without doubt been offended by the idea. The views from the car park lookout are beautiful and you can see all the way up to Kingsbridge in the far distance and down onto Salcombe itself where hundreds of small boats are moored, sheltered from the open sea. Celebrities, such as Kate Bush, Michael Parkinson and Steve Rider reportedly have second homes in East Portlemouth and since in the 2011 census the total population of the village was only 162 then I guess that indigenous residents might well be outnumbered by celebrities.

East Portlemouth ferry.

Leaving the heights we then followed a typically narrow lane down to the waters edge where a completely different perspective of the estuary could be gained. The majority of visitors to this area of South Devon are primarily attracted to Salcombe that lies on the opposite side of the water. However there is a small passenger ferry that will transport an adult at a cost of £1.70 in each direction from 8.00 a.m. until 17.30 p.m. throughout the year. Woe betide any visitor to East Portlemouth who misses the last ferry back to Salcombe, although perhaps Kate, Michael or Steve might put them up for the night.

There seemed to be very few other options to stay in East Portlemouth although I did find an Airbnb that sleeps nine at a very reasonable £1,000 per night! East Portlemouth is known for the clean estuary water and safe sandy beaches although somehow looking directly out over urban Salcombe didn't have the same attraction for me as looking out to sea, however golden the sands might be. The small Venus Cafe is conveniently situated above the slipway and the ferry was continuously shuttling back and forth. After the obligatory coffee and cake it was time for us to leave East Portlemouth and we had already identified a promising route back to Frogmore that ran close to the waters edge along Southpool Creek and then on to South Pool. The route most certainly did not disappoint and although three fords had to be crossed the tide was fortunately out. Occasionally very impressive houses could just be seen hidden by trees and after passing through the aptly named

South Pool.

Goodshelter the village of South Pool finally came into sight. What caught my eye on entering South Pool was the lovely old stone bridge upon which a lifebelt hung ready for any emergency. The written instructions were perfectly clear, namely to ring 999 for the Coastguard should that be necessary. The fact that the water beneath the bridge was only a few inches deep at the time seemed to make the instruction somewhat excessive.

Millbrook Inn.

Although I was previously unaware of the fact in 2022 the Conde Naste magazine placed South Pool in the top twenty prettiest locations to visit in the UK and Ireland. How the shortlist was derived and who made the final selection I have no idea but from my personal experience I would say that such a list is fairly meaningless because we have hundreds of the 'prettiest' villages spread throughout the land. I later read that the Millbrook Inn in South Pool is a well respected gastropub that reportedly *'fuses English pub grub with French cuisine'*. The sample dinner menu certainly looked enticing but I may have to save up a little longer for 'Bangers and Mash' at £19.00 and a starter of 'Pig's head rissole' for

£10.00 didn't really do it for me. Nevertheless one day I will return to the Millbrook Inn to eat but now it was time for us to head on home.

Chapter 23
Old John

Old John Thompson slowly pushed his council barrow down the Emerson Street pedestrian precinct. At set intervals he would stop, remove the appropriate sized broom, and clean up any rubbish from the adjacent area. His barrow was currently a sight to behold since he had recently modified it himself in order to be able to more efficiently separate the plastic from the bottles from the paper and so on. Along either side of the barrow he had attached fixings for his shovel, dust pan and brush, chewing gum scraper and so on. It was a veritable Christmas tree of gadgets to assist his occupation as street sweeper, or what the council now officially called, Environmental Health Officer, Grade Four. As far as John was concerned he was still a simple street sweeper and had been so for the last forty years. Napier City centre was his patch and it always had been.

Every Tuesday and Thursday he made a particular point of cleaning up outside of the Court House on Hastings Street. He would often see familiar young faces waiting for their turn to face the magistrate. He had seen their fathers and mothers before them.

'Hello Tommy, what's it this time?'

'Oh I just got bored again Mr Thompson. We don't have any facilities in Onekawa like those posh folks in Taradale and Murawai have. Community centres, sports grounds and all that.'

'Perhaps that's because you always smash them up Tommy.'

'No we don't Mr Thompson. They're just not made very well, that's all.'

'There's a lot of truth in that Tommy. Perhaps they'll get it right for you all the next time. How's your dad?'

'Aw he's sweet. Haven't seen him for a few months, but he's sweet. He's got a job working in the mill at Tokaroa.'

'Glad to hear it Tommy. He is a good man your dad. Just made a few mistakes when he was young.'

Occasionally there were groups outside of the court that John didn't recognise and sometimes they would take pleasure abusing him as he tried to do his job.

'What the fuck do you want you old bastard' they would often say as they refused to step aside in order that he could clean the pavement where they were standing.

'Hello son,' John would respond in a kindly manner. 'I'm just trying to make the street clean for you all. You know, tidy up and that.'

Somehow they didn't seem to have any response to this. They could see that he had no fear. They were just used to confrontation, of facing up, of not ever backing down. And before long they took to the old man in the royal blue shirt, black shorts and wide rimmed hat. And then it was 'G'day Mr Thompson,' and before long they would confide in him, look for his guidance, accept the wisdom of an elder, even if he were not of their particular 'iwi'.

And it was the same with everyone that John encountered on his rounds. He always had time for a chat and they with him. Once, a few years ago, the council assigned a time and motion man to follow John around for a week. At the end of the first day the man was exhausted. On the second day John just said, 'Why don't you just go and have a coffee. Life's too short to get too stressed.' On the third day they both sat down in the park and had a laugh while they filled in all seven days of the form in one go.

'Satisfactory, alright for you John? We don't want to overdo it.'

'That'll be just fine Jim.'

And that's how it was. Everyone knew John, and John knew everyone. The shopkeepers loved him for keeping their areas so clean and tidy. The tourists observed him as he quietly pottered around the streets just doing his job.

'But it's bloody council property Murray' said Councillor Robinson. 'You can't just let people do what they like. We'll have police cars with fairy lights on soon.'

'Come off it Fred. John's always used his initiative and the streets are spotless. Always have been. You've seen how residents are reluctant to drop litter in case they set a bad example. You won't see that in Wellington or Auckland.'

John was a regular topic of conversation at the council meetings. Most of the discussions related to his age and pending retirement.

'Let's face it Murray, John is getting on. We've been talking about making him take retirement for the last ten years. For God's sake he must be seventy five by now.'

'Seventy four Fred. And you won't find a more conscientious worker this side of the dateline. Never had a sick note in all the years I've been on the council and he does a damn good job. You can't deny it'

'We all know that Murray,' said the Mayor, 'but the budget is tight and we have to make cuts. So what's the latest on the Suton SupaSweeper, Fred?'

'Well the consultants have finally delivered their report and it all looks good. Capital cost of the self-propelled model is seventy five thousand bucks and they work out that it will save us twenty thousand in staff costs per year, net. Pay for itself and more in four or so years.'

'You saw the bloody thing Fred. Pissing all over the place, flashing lights and frightening the locals and visitors to death. Does it really need to have that high pitched bleeper sounding off all of the ruddy time?'

'Health and safety Murray,' Fred responded helpfully. 'Can't afford to be sued by some American lawyer off one of the cruise ships.'

'But it doesn't even do a good job. It can't handle the bollards, it can't sweep up in the nooks and crannies. It can't clean up dog mess. Basically it is C.R.A.P.'

'We know it's not as good as a human operative,' continued Fred 'but we have to move with the times. You just can't stand still. It's called progress Murray.'

'Is that so. Well you know where you can stick your progress Fred.'

'Calm down. Calm down,' said the Mayor. 'Why the hell whenever John's name comes up do we always have to have a blazing row. Let's just grow up. Perhaps if we give him a long service certificate and a clock he will be happy to retire on his seventy fifth?'

'He's already had two of both,' said Murray.

'Alright' said the Mayor. 'How many votes for John to be given one more year. Right. Carried. Thank God for that. Now let's get on to some more important business.'

At the end of the working day John would empty his barrow contents into the appropriate skips and park it in the council shed located directly behind the police station. He would then make his way along Shakespeare Road, then France Road and on up the hill to the very end of Elizabeth Road, where he lived. On numerous occasions people offered to give him a lift to his home to save him the climb but he always refused saying that the exercise did him good, as if the ten kilometres he walked each working day were not enough. The climb would draw the breath from all but the very fittest and John was certainly no different. In the summer heat it was particularly difficult but the shade of the occasional overhanging trees offered some respite. Usually he would do one hundred steps at a time and then rest for a minute or so whilst exchanging greetings with the familiar faces going up or down. Finally he would reach his destination.

To the casual observer the small cottage where he lived was typical of its type, if somewhat dilapidated compared to others in the vicinity. He had lived in this house ever since he was born, all those years ago. Somehow the salary of a street sweeper had not allowed him to maintain it to a certain standard in the early years but perhaps that is what now gave it so much character. Very few people had had cause to visit his home in the past and perhaps that was because he valued his privacy so very highly. Few even knew where he lived and only the council and taxman had cause to know his actual address for official correspondence.

Five years ago the two sections next to his had been sold and a single magnificent contemporary dwelling had been constructed behind high wooden fences and an electric gate guaranteed to keep out strangers. On occasion he would encounter Mrs Potts, who lived directly opposite his cottage, who believed that she had the right to know the business of every one of her neighbours. John excepted of course.

'I saw the Porsche four wheel drive leave last weekend John,' she would say. 'You know the one with the dark tinted windows. Mabel said they must be foreigners since any Kiwi would have made themselves known to their neighbours by now. Perhaps film stars of some sort? Don't you think so John?'

'I guess that you're right Joan,' was all that John would say. 'Beautiful evening, don't you think? and with that he unlatched his wooden gate and made his way to his front door. Internally his home confirmed it's external appearance. Little would appear to have changed since his parents had lived there all those years ago and that was just how he had always liked it. Even some of the furnishings were original, including the grandfather clock.

John was a man of habit and the first thing that he did on arriving home was to place his work clothes into the old fashioned top loading washing machine. Switching it on he would then proceed to lay out his neatly ironed work clothes for the following day on his spare bed. He would then clean his boots so that they reflected the scene as clearly as a mirror and next he would draw his bath, filling it to the overflow with steaming hot water. He would wash his hair in the bath using an old tin dog bowl, lie back and just soak for at least twenty minutes. Occasionally he would add more hot water to suit by turning the tap on and off with his big toe.

Feeling much refreshed he would then dress, shorts and a short sleeved shirt in the summer, slip on his jandals and enter the enclosed garden by the back door, locking it securely behind him. A dilapidated tool shed covered in ivy abutted the neighbouring fence and on entering inside he closed the door firmly behind him. On the back wall a tall cupboard full of garden tools stood and this he moved aside with ease since it was mounted on rails. Within a few seconds he had entered another tool shed, but this was of much finer quality, being made of imported English oak. It just so happened that it was located in the neighbouring property. Then reaching inside the pocket of his shorts he would retrieve the electronic key and enter the mansion on the ground floor.

The contemporary design was in complete contrast to the home that he had just left. Clean neutral colour walls with abstract paintings of vivid reds, greens and blues. A short ride in a futuristic lift took him soundlessly from the basement to a second floor which was flooded with the westerly light of the evening sun. Triple glazed sliding glass windows extended from floor to ceiling on the other side of the house offering unobstructed easterly panoramic views from the Mahia Peninsula to Cape Kidnappers. There was no finer house in the city and he knew them all. And it was all his.

It is strange how fate takes a hand in life. Fifty years before he had spent his usual dollar on the weekly lottery and then one day he had hit 'pay dirt'. Well one thousand dollars was an awful lot in those days. But he had not spent the money because he had everything that he needed in his cottage on Elizabeth Road. He had kept knowledge of his win to himself since he was quite happy in his work and he needed little else. He had always been particularly careful with his money and therefore his windfall had encouraged him develop a new interest in finance and investment. The ladies at the Napier City Library sometimes ribbed him as he withdrew some financial tome or another but he just responded by saying that he had a wonky table at home and a good book solved all of his problems. The only problem he said was that he had to keep returning the book and take out another. There you go they said to one another. That's our John for you.

And then one day he came across an up and coming investment company and he finally made the decision where the home for his windfall would be. Over the years his investment grew in an unbelievable way and he could have retired many years ago a wealthy man. But he loved his work and the people that he met every day. They were almost family. Giving up the streets would have been the early death of him, that's for sure. So he hired a Wellington lawyer and formed a charitable trust on the understanding that he would remain totally anonymous. The JT Charitable Trust it was called.

The projects closest to his heart were related to the troubled youths and families that he came across outside of the court house every week of the year. And so as finances allowed the Trust would support the construction of community and sports facilities in the Napier area. First it had been Tamatea, then Muruwai, then Napier South and next it would be Onekawa. Occasionally he would drive out at weekends in his Porsche with tinted windows closed just to see the community facilities that he had financed. But more importantly he would observe the body language of the young people who were entering and leaving the facilities that he had built. It was fulfilment personified. He never left his Porsche. Simply observed.

The mansion on the hill with the spectacular views was just his little indulgence. But leave work as a street cleaner. Not in his lifetime, at least voluntarily. And you can't have street cleaners arriving for work in a Porsche and living in mansions can you. And so as far as the council were concerned it was Old John who lived in his little cottage on the hill.

That evening he sat there on the balcony of his mansion gazing out to the far horizon, master of all he surveyed. And raising his glass of chilled Marlborough sauvignon blanc he said out loud, 'Your very good health Mr Buffet. Your very good health Mr Munger. Berkshire Hathaway have done Napier and myself proud.'

Trevor Cree
2012

Chapter 24
Start Point & Beesands

Friday, 16th September 2022

After my previous debacle I was determined to make it all the way to Start Point this time, just as Captain Scott and his team had made it all the way to the South Pole. However, on reflection, that was a pretty poor analogy in view of the tragic outcome of their own expedition. As always I tried to avoid the main roads because a moped and high speed traffic just do not mix. After reaching Frogmore I therefore took the familiar narrow lane to South Pool and then cut across country to South Allington, as originally intended. At least I think that I went through South Allington but, as is the case with so many hamlets in South Devon, it was so small that I hardly noticed. Fortunately a signpost to Start Point soon appeared at a road junction and it was smooth sailing all the way after that.

Start Bay.

The car park attendant at Start Point was very friendly and it must be quite some job when the gales howl across the exposed peninsula. The path to the lighthouse drops a considerable height offering beautiful views across Start Bay to the 'lost village' of Hallsands, right up to Beesands and beyond. After the trek down it was actually a disappointment to be faced with a large impersonal locked gate and to be truthful not a particularly good view of the lighthouse. However I had previously noticed what appeared to be a route up to the bluff that overlooked the lighthouse and this could be reached by holding on to a steel chain ropeway that was clearly of ancient vintage.

The challenge was too great to resist and so going hand over hand I finally reached the top. The view down to the lighthouse and out to sea was now magnificent but the drop from where I stood was sheer all the way down to the sea below. Nevertheless, as Edmund Hillary famously said after climbing Everest, 'We knocked the bastard off'. I had thought that the rusty old steel chain was an authorised route but as bits of chain came away from the earth on my descent I soon realised that was probably not the case. However mission accomplished it was then back to the car park and onwards to the lost village of Hallsands.

Lost village of Hallsands.

It would seem that there had been a chapel in Hallsands ever since 1506 but it was only in the 18th and 19th century that the settlement grew in size until it contained 37 houses and even a public house named the London Inn. It was a very close knit community where the residents depended on fishing for a living, particularly crab. In the 1890s sand and gravel was dredged offshore by the authorities to assist in the expansion of the naval dockyard in Plymouth, much to the residents dismay. An inquiry was set up that concluded that the dredging was not likely to have any impact on the village. However the dredging licence was revoked in 1902 but by then the irreversible damage to the settlement had been done. In fact by 1917 only one house remained habitable but its occupant, Elizabeth Prettyjohn, stubbornly refused to leave and amazingly she lived there with her chickens until her death in 1964. The ruined village itself is closed to the public because of the unstable cliffs but a viewing platform has been constructed so that all can see the result of man's folly when natural resources are over exploited.

Beesands.

A little further up the coast sits Beesands and as usual it was quite a task finding it along very narrow lanes. However once reached it is a really charming little fishing village, even if the gigantic rocks in the sea wall bear witness to the battering it must take during the winter storms. It has no harbour as such and therefore the small but colourful fishing boats are pulled up on to the shingle beach, well above the high water line.

A poem on the sea wall fondly remembers a local man who lost his life but how he died is unstated.

Wayne 1968 - 2020

*Standing off the solid stone steps
or from the pebbled shore
where you have fished
and made us proud more
than a thousand times before.
Stay close Wayne xxxx*

Fishing boats, Beesands.

The Cricket Inn pub looked very welcoming but I decided to indulge in a crab sandwich from the nearby Britannia at the Beach. A Union Jack at half mast, somewhat weather worn, fluttered in the breeze in recognition of our Queen Elizabeth II who had recently passed away after a lifetime of service. The adjacent fishing gear, hanging on a steel rail, gave the flag a poignant and appropriate setting. Overall it had been a very successful outing but it was now time to return to my little 'home in the country'.

Union Jack at half mast at Beesands.

Chapter 25
Bluff Hill

At the same time every day a solitary figure stood leaning against the top rail of a wire mesh fence at the eastern margins of the Bluff Hill lookout. It was as if he were looking for the arrival of a ship from a far off land. A ship which never came and which would never come. For hours he would gaze out to the horizon oblivious to the comings and goings of the local residents and tourists who stayed for just a while to admire the panoramic view.

Below the cliff face the port of Napier hummed with industrious activity. Ocean going ships yielded up their cargos in exchange for apples, wine, lamb, lumber and newly slain deer. From the elevated vantage point visitors could observe minute figures going about their routine port duties. The man in the white boiler suit checking the anchor motors and capstans; two others sitting precariously on a dangling plank painting the ship's side; the navigating officer observing the cargo movements from the bridge.

Alongside Kirkpatrick Wharf another ship lay higher than a ten story building as cranes removed and replaced containers guided by some unfathomable mathematical equation. Giant fork lift trucks raised containers from the quay as if they contained feathers and transported them to some predetermined storage area or directly onto trucks for immediate dispatch to some unknown destination. The activities of a world of barter and exchange continued unaffected by the days, by the months, by the years.

The route that the man took to the lookout never varied. Leaving the modest room that he rented in Sale Street he would make his way across the road to the seaward side of Marine Parade. The recently constructed beach path would then be his route north with the occasional greeting exchanged with fellow walkers, cyclists and young skate boarders. Sometimes the surf would pound the fine black sand, sometimes the water would simply lap the shore, sometimes a cool wind would blow from the south. And then the strenuous part of his journey would begin with the steepening incline of Coote Road before he took the shortcut up a concrete path located at the end of Priestley Road. Then into Lighthouse Road and finally the narrow winding walk to the Bluff itself.

Such a daily climb would be considered invigorating by many but the man was neither as young nor as active as the majority of those who walked up to the lookout by alternative paths. His snow white hair indicated an age well in excess of sixty years and his laboured gait would have offered further confirmation of the same. It was a daily journey that he had been making for nearly one month now and the approach of Christmas was signalled by the flowering of the pohutukawa trees.

He was not naturally gregarious by nature and had become protective of his favoured position on the hill that he seemed to have made his own. At least for a few hours every day. It was therefore with irritation that he found on one particular day that his spot, his sacred spot, had been occupied by a young woman prior to his arrival. He had fully expected her to stay for just a short time, as was the normal pattern, after which he could reclaim his rightful place. But she just stayed until late in the afternoon and he had to occupy a less favoured vantage point. He resolved to arrive earlier the following morning to reclaim his right and this he successfully achieved.

He had only been settled in his place for a few minutes when he heard the light steps of someone approaching from behind. He turned with the uncharitable intention of giving the intruder of his personal space a territorial glare. Before him stood a young women of Asian appearance, of slight build and short in stature. Her disarming smile had an immediate soothing effect on his ill humour and any thought of annoyance departed on the soft warm breeze.

'Hello,' she said. 'Do you mind if I share the view? It is such a good location.'

Her English was impeccable but he had difficulty identifying her exact origins on the global map. He thought that she could possibly be from Hong Kong since he knew how precisely the schools there ingrained the Queen's English into their pupils.

'No, not at all,' he replied, somewhat untruthfully.

They stood in close proximity to each other, without conversing, for a full fifteen minutes. For a time each was occupied by their own private thoughts but now those thoughts had become hopelessly distracted by the immediate presence of the other. Neither could reach the state of quiet contemplation where each needed to be. At last the man could bear the silence no longer.

'Are you on vacation in New Zealand?' he said searching hesitantly for some neutral ground.

'No, not exactly,' she replied. 'Are you?'

'No, not exactly? So perhaps you are studying in New Zealand or visiting relations then?' he continued, working on a simple process of elimination.

'No', she replied. She looked at him thoughtfully for a while. Her eyes saw an old man in clothes of fine quality but now somewhat threadbare. A man who had seen better days. A man of kindly features. A man that she sensed that she could confide in and she desperately needed to confide in someone.

'Since you asked me a direct question I am actually seeking political asylum,' she said. She looked at him for any kind of negative reaction but he simply smiled. He did not respond to her words but looked wistfully out to sea. And so she continued.

'My name is Han Julin. I'm Chinese. I'm originally from Chengdu in Szechuan province. I later studied mathematics in Beijing at Qinghua University for five years. It is one of China's very best universities you know. I love my country but I now have to make my home in New Zealand.'

'Forgive me,' he continued, 'but China has flourished over the last fifteen years or more. Young people like yourself appear to have great opportunities to succeed, to create their own businesses, to own their own homes, to travel overseas. Why would you want to leave and give all that up for an uncertain future in a distant land?'

'I think that it is difficult for a foreigner to understand. You only see the wide range of inexpensive Chinese products in your shops; the massive skyscrapers soaring to the sky in Shanghai, Guangdong and Beijing, the Olympic games so efficiently organised; KFC and MacDonalds on every corner; smiling officials shaking hands with your leaders, kowtowing with equal enthusiasm. You do not know the language. You have not seen the fear in peoples eyes. You cannot understand the massive weight of the Party bearing down on peoples shoulders, crushing them slowly, completely, remorselessly. Can you?'

'No. Indeed I cannot. Please continue.'

'When I was very young I was on a train entering Beijing. It was late afternoon. The train had halted for a short while on a bridge overlooking one of the new highways. The road was full of thousands upon thousands of people walking en masse towards the centre of the city. I asked my father what was going on, was there some wonderful celebration happening, would there be fireworks. My father looked at me and smiled, 'Yes, my daughter, it is a festival.' But his face was sad and I saw tears in his eyes. We returned unexpectedly to Chengdu the very next day. My father said that he had urgent business to attend to at the factory where he worked as a senior manager. I was too young to understand but we were later informed at elementary school that a great victory had been won by the people, reactionary elements had been defeated. We children were all so happy but my own family were subdued, quiet.'

'It was only much later, when I travelled to Hong Kong with the university that I fully understood. Again there were masses of people marching, smiling people and banners with slogans such as 'Freedom' and 'Democracy Now'. And the police were good humoured and did not intervene. People were allowed to protest against their government. It was such a shock. I did not see the police seize demonstrators and take them up dark alleyways for interrogation. But I still saw the plain clothes thugs, far smaller in number it is true, but so recognisable. It was if they were saying, 'Not now, but we are patient, we can wait, our time will come.' And I could see that beneath the Hong Kong veneer of normality an ugly force still reigned supreme. A force that could never be defeated. It was clear to me that there would never be true freedom anywhere in China during my lifetime. There would never be democracy. I would never be able to stand at the Gates of Heaven and openly express my opposition to government policies as I could in Hong Kong. And so from that point on I quietly planned for freedom. I chose life. I chose liberty.'

'After Tiananmen my father had changed. It was as if he had concluded that the only way to protect his family was to out cadre the cadres and rise in the ranks of the city and then provincial committees. Sometimes I heard him quietly discussing this with my mother in the next room. My father is a very hard working man when most party leaders are not and he soon rose in the hierarchy due to his ability.

However his easy going character dramatically changed and his tone became more strident and dictatorial. He was no longer the father that I knew as a child and we steadily grew apart. Sometimes, in unguarded moments, I saw a great sadness in his eyes but that was soon replaced by a coldness and rigid determination. He had chosen a path and that he would follow.'

'But why have you applied for asylum. I don't understand why that is necessary?' the old man asked.

'The 18th National Congress of the Chinese Communist Party has only recently ended and my father was one of the delegates. The congress resulted in the quiet expulsion of large numbers of party members due to corruption but my father had always been scrupulously honest. Unexpected openings therefore arose for promotion to the Central Committee and because my father had shown absolute loyalty to the party, and in particular to Xi Jinping, he was elected. It was a great honour of course for our family but for me it finally signalled the end. I could never accept the thought of seeing my father on television screens clapping in unison with two thousand other delegates like mindless smiling automatons. My worst fears had been realised. It was as if my father had died and I was no longer his daughter.'

'And so at the end of November I immediately booked a flight and travelled to New Zealand on a tourist visa but as soon as I arrived I sought asylum. It was a country that I had studied deeply and always admired. I cannot say that my application was warmly greeted by the authorities at immigration but I suppose that is to be expected. I have been told that I will receive the final decision on my application on the tenth of January.'

'But why did you not simply apply to migrate here? You are young, intelligent, clearly very highly qualified and just the sort of person that this country is currently welcoming from China in their thousands?'

'I know that very well,' she replied. 'It is complicated. Migration was never a viable option for me personally because my father is now one of the top two hundred party members in China. Can you imagine that, with a population of over 1.3 billion people and my father is one of the elite.

The children of high ranking members cannot be seen to be forfeiting their Chinese nationality and adopting foreign citizenship. Their children are certainly welcome to create businesses in foreign countries, flaunt their obscene wealth and drive their Ferraris but they can never renounce their Chinese nationality. Never. To do so would reflect very badly on the Central Committee members whose own loyalty to China would then be seriously questioned.'

'Migration applications have to be completed in the country of origin and so formal migration was never a viable option for me. New Zealand requires references from the Chinese authorities in relation to character and previous criminal convictions and I know that false accusations would have been made against me to thwart my application. And I would never have been told the reason why, just an official rejection from the New Zealand embassy in Beijing. End of story. And so you see I had no other option but to apply for asylum as soon as I had landed in New Zealand.'

'You know that you will not be successful,' the old man said without emotion. 'Politics and trade are uneasy bedfellows with democracy and human rights. There are too many vested interests, whether politically or financially. New Zealand has come to depend almost totally on China ever since access to the EU markets was effectively closed many years ago.'

'It is true that there are far greater forces at work than ourselves' she responded. 'I had just hoped, naively it is true, I had just hoped that New Zealand was different. That they could accept me for what I am, a simple person striving to be free. No more, no less. Should that not be enough? But what about you? What is your story?'

'I am also seeking refuge,' he replied, 'but in a different sort of way.'

She looked at him closely. Her intellectual mind was processing the information before her and no matter which way she computed it the result never came out as refugee. It came out as English, it came out as European, it came out as American, it came out as free, but never as someone such as herself desperately seeking refuge.

'Sorry, I think that I must have misunderstood what you said. Did you say that you were also seeking refuge or was I mistaken? Perhaps it was your way to humour me? Perhaps to make fun of me?'

'No, neither to humour nor to make fun of you. I would never do that. I am a seeker of refuge but as I said in a particular sort of way. I can fully understand your doubting my claim but you see, like yourself, I now have no other place to go. Like yourself I can no longer bear to live in my home country. My claim for permanent residence in New Zealand is currently under review before my visa expires. I have little realistic hope for it to be granted because I am now too old, without the right qualifications or skills, without the necessary funds to invest, without close relations who live here. A potential future burden on the health service and on social care. I have to accept that but I just have to try because I cannot return to England. I will also be informed about their decision on the tenth of January. It must be a very auspicious date.'

'Indeed it must be' she said. 'How very strange.'

He paused for a moment and then carried on.

'It is difficult to explain but I hope that you will understand. My country, England, has only recently commenced the same journey that China has already travelled but it has. When I was a young man my country was a land of hope and opportunity. The war in Europe had just ended and the future could be viewed with real optimism. Like everyone else my parents had very little but there was real freedom and community. Governments came and departed, always changing each others policies, unions struck and workers took to the streets, power cuts came and went, but it was a real, vibrant society. At the time there were numerous ways for young people to progress with free access to university or college, based on merit and not on wealth or patronage. Apprenticeships in all sorts of trades were available producing skilled workers for building a better tomorrow. Our democratic votes actually counted for something. We therefore had some influence over the future direction of the country.'

'And so I took advantage of all of the opportunities open to me, married and divorced, quietly living my life, just voting as and when required, but totally apolitical. But then things changed. Imperceptibly at first. It was the very early nineties. The grey men and women of newspeak started to infiltrate the structures of power. You have to admire their perseverance and patience. Even now most of my compatriots are unaware of the fact and even if they were aware they probably would not object. Just as long as nothing directly impacted on their daily lives and what they could happily absorb from the television screen with its hundred channels and more.'

'I find it hard to believe you', she said. 'The home of modern democracy? The mother of parliaments?' But then she looked at him and knew that what he said was true. There was a pause and then he continued.

'I fully understand your doubting what I say. Who would not. But if you lived in England you might understand more. The steady erosion of our freedoms, the Orwellian banality of the radio and television programmes, the unfulfilled promises on education, pensions, housing, health and social care. The incessant repetitive brainwashing of commercial advertising, the subtle increase in surveillance, the collapse of community and family, the indoctrination of our children from a very early age, the banality of it all. And now it makes no difference what party is in power in my country. They are all professional politicians who have no experience of the lives of ordinary people and they have no wish to know.'

'But you live in a democracy', she said. 'Why did you not stand up and oppose those forces?'

'But I did' he said. 'I did just that for ten years. Firstly I stood for our local council in the naive belief that I could make an impact at the grassroots level. Failing to achieve anything there I then stood as an Independent for the district council and was elected. But I was just one voice against many, each with their narrow political affiliations, each just putting their hands in the air like zombies as instructed. Whatever the soundness of the case, however compelling the argument, the outcome was just the same. And when you spoke to your own constituents it was to be met with understandable cynicism but most disappointing of all was the apathy. It was if everyone was on medication of some kind.'

'One morning two years ago I looked in the mirror and I saw a very old and tired man looking back at me. And so I decided that I had to make a drastic change in my life before I ended up as cynical and apathetic as everyone else. I had realised that the country that I had loved so deeply all my life no longer existed. I was a stranger in my own land. I could not live out the remainder of my days gradually getting more and more embittered, resentful and angry. The only place where I had found peace in the past was New Zealand, a country that I had visited a number of times and had rapidly fallen in love with. I had no roots there, no relations there but then I no longer had roots anywhere. Those roots had simply withered and died. And so I cannot contemplate ever returning to England and I have nowhere else that I want to go or can go at my age. For me it has to be New Zealand or nowhere.'

'Thank you for explaining your situation so clearly' she said. 'I now understand your utter despair and how similar it is to mine. Like yourself I know in my heart that my application for asylum will be rejected. On the tenth of January we will both know our fate.'

'This will be as good a place to meet as anywhere?' he said.

'Indeed it will' she replied.

And with that both looked over the fence at the sheer drop of two hundred feet below. Yes. It would indeed be an appropriate place to meet.

Trevor Cree
2012

Chapter 26
Errrr-mington

Friday, 23rd September 2022

Since the late summer days were passing rather quickly I decided to make the most of the recently improved weather and undertake a short outing to the village of Ermington. I was already familiar with a significant part of the route because those were the very lanes that I took when travelling to Ivybridge for the monthly South Hams Authors Network meetings at the Imperial Inn. I set off in high anticipation because Ermington was the home of a church with a crooked spire, the predictably named Crooked Spire pub, the 'First and Last' bistro and perhaps much more.

The hamlet of Sheepham was soon passed and then Rucio and I took a left turn along Ridge Road which offered magnificent views across the valley to Modbury that was rapidly receding into the distance. Ridge Road got narrower and narrower whilst the earth banks got higher and higher and worryingly there were very limited places to pass. Fortunately we never did meet any other vehicle on the whole descent and after reaching a main road I knew that we simply had to take a left and within a short distance Ermington would soon appear on the right. The distance along the main road to the village was further than I had anticipated but at long last a church spire came into view and we duly took a right up Church Lane until the back gate of the churchyard was finally located.

Gravestone.

A beautifully engraved 1791 gravestone stood beside the church footpath and it was remarkable how the precise script had remained so legible after 231 years. The graveyard grass had recently been cut and a path led lower down the slope to a location that seemed to offer an excellent position where I could take a photograph of the famous crooked spire. The spire did not look crooked from that particular angle but I concluded that it would become more pronounced depending on where you were actually standing within the churchyard. On entering the church itself through a very rickety door it became immediately apparent that there was an absence of stained glass within that gave a sense of cold rather than warmth to the interior. Nevertheless the view looking directly down the aisle to the altar was magnificent.

It was then time to set about exploring the village of Ermington itself and I took a short walk to what appeared to be the main street. A cottage painted pink reminded me very much of one that I had seen in Modbury and perhaps there might be a general preference for pastel colours in South Devon. Rather than continue on foot I decided to return to the church to take Rucio to the village centre.

We descended a very steep hill and on reaching the bottom I looked around for a place to park and it was then that I noticed a Modbury Community notice board and the rear of the White Hart Hotel. Nothing particularly unusual about that, apart from the fact that the White Hart Hotel is in Modbury and not Ermington!

Church spire.

There was absolutely no doubt about it in my mind and there could be no other logical explanation. I had somehow been teleported from the centre of Ermington to the centre of Modbury in a millisecond. All those years that I had watched Star Trek and had seen Captain Kirk and Doctor Spock teleporting themselves throughout time and space I had simply thought that it was entertaining science fiction. But now it had actually happened to me. It was a very very strange and inexplicable experience.

Slowly, too slowly some might say, it dawned on me that I had not been teleported anywhere at all. It was simply a case that the lanes of South Devon had once again played tricks on me. Ridge Road was not the route that I should have taken to Ermington at all because it actually ran parallel to and inexorably away from the village the further I travelled along it. I was correct to turn left when reaching the main road but it just happened to be the wrong main road!

In my defence none of the places that I had seen after my unintended arrival in Modbury had seemed at all familiar until I finally came to be sitting at the rear of the White Hart Hotel. It was all very embarrassing but there was nothing that I could do but go to the Co-op, go home and try again another day. In football terms it was clearly South Devon Lanes 6 - Sussex Simpleton 0. Fortunately if I never tell anyone then nobody will ever know.

Chapter 27
Mountain Flower

High above the barren plateau,
Set among the rock strewn plain,
Covered round with thorny bushes,
Grew a lonely mountain flower.
Autumn, winter, spring and summer,
Sun and snow, hail and rain,
Brightly coloured petals did issue,
From the solitary green refrain.
Old men said it was a miracle,
Mandarins passed with disdain,
Peasants tied their silken ribbons,
To surrounding bushes plain.
As the seasons passed one to the other,
As the decades slipped away,
Mountain flowers grew in number,
Spreading each and every way.
Soon the landscape filled with colour,
Brightly shining blossoms all,
Children could but scarce remember,
When it were but dark grey pall.
High above the barren plateau,
Set among the rock strewn plain,
Covered round with thorny bushes,
Grew a lonely mountain flower.

Trevor Cree
China 1990

Chapter 28
Ermington

Saturday, 24th September 2022

After yesterday's teleporting fiasco I was determined to get it right this time and the journey to the village of Ermington went without a hitch. As soon as the crooked spire of St Peter & St Paul came into view I knew that Rucio and I were finally in the right place. I found a convenient parking spot right outside of the Crooked Spire Inn but then, disaster. The pub didn't open until 5.00 pm and, although I only ever have a single pint, a drink and the pub atmosphere is always one of the highlights of any visit.

The local records state that in 1856 the spire of St Peter & Paul was struck by lightening and the vicar felt that that was an ideal opportunity to finally rebuild a straight spire. However the people of the parish protested that the spire had always been crooked and it was clearly meant to be so, and that is how it has remained until this day.

The interior of the church was an unexpected surprise in so many ways, not least because of the beautiful wooden carvings that were created by three local women. Mary, Ethel and Violet Pinwill were the daughters of the Reverend Edmund Pinwill, vicar of Ermington at that time, and his wife Elizabeth Greatorex.

Ermington church pulpit.

Now Greatorex is a very interesting name, so similar in my mind to Asterix the Gaul, but in fact it is of Anglo-Saxon origin and is primarily associated with lead mining in Derbyshire. During the restoration of the church Elizabeth asked the head of the restoration carving team to teach her young daughters wood carving. Three of the girls subsequently became professional woodcarvers in an age when that profession was almost exclusively undertaken by men.

Their pulpit carving received great acclaim and by 1890 the sisters had set up their own Rashleigh, Pinwill & Co. workshop in Plymouth that had been so named to hide the fact that the owners and carvers were actually women. The impressive altar, that incorporates the nativity scene in carved stone, was the sole work of Violet Pinwell.

Ermington church altar.

Walking beyond the church in the Ivybridge direction I found, by chance, the 'Store and More' cafe, gift shop and community hub. It offered a variety of hot and cold snacks and it seemed only right that I should support such a local initiative and buy something to eat and drink. I wasn't particularly hungry and so the special offer of crumpets, butter, jam and tea for £3 seemed to fit the bill. It appeared that the cafe owner's children were helping out for the day and so I placed my order with the boy who appeared to be about eleven years old. He dutifully entered the items in the till one by one until he said 'That will be £2 please'. I pointed to the special offer £3 sign on the table and happily gave him the correct amount to which he simply said, 'Thank you very much.' Although the adding up left a little to be desired it was really encouraging to see two youngsters gaining an understanding of business, something that I never achieved. One part of 'Store and More' was specifically set aside as the community hub where local groups could meet, including the youth and dance clubs.

'Store and More' community hub cafe.

In view of its architecture the adjacent 'First and Last' bistro looked to have been a pub at some time in the past but perhaps I was mistaken. It was good to see that the traditional Sunday lunch was on the menu and that it included a choice of roast chicken, pork, lamb and beef, in other words the full monty of choice. The evening menu also looked enticing whilst the wines were reasonably priced for the reasonably well heeled, among whom I do not currently consider myself. Nevertheless I was still able to savour the content of the menu if not the actual product.

The First & Last Bistro.

About the Author

Trevor Cree was born in Steyning, Sussex, and has lived there most of his life. He studied agricultural engineering at the University of Newcastle upon Tyne and spent his professional career working in over 30 countries worldwide undertaking short-term consultancy assignments for various international entities, including the UN Food and Agriculture Organization (FAO), European Union (EU) and UN High Commissioner for Refugees (UNHCR). Travel to countries such as China, North Korea, Vietnam, Sudan, Yemen, Iraq, Iran, Syria, Moldova, Albania, Liberia and Sierra Leone influenced his views on the importance of democracy and democratic accountability. From 2012 onwards he took an active part in parish council affairs in Steyning in an effort to increase openness and transparency in local government.

'Modbury Tales' was written during an eight month stay in South Devon in 2022 and subsequently published as an eBook. In 2025 'Modbury Tales' was republished in the current paperback format.

Books by the same Author

Track (2005)

Random Journeys - New Zealand (2011)

The Writer's Diary (2022)

The Clock Tower Affair (2025)

Printed in Dunstable, United Kingdom